Groundwater Quality in Central New York, 2007

By David A.V. Eckhardt, J.E. Reddy, and Stephen B. Shaw

Prepared in cooperation with the
New York State Department of Environmental Conservation

Open-File Report 2009-1257

U.S. Department of the Interior
U.S. Geological Survey

U.S. Department of the Interior
KEN SALAZAR, Secretary

U.S. Geological Survey
Marcia K. McNutt, Director

U.S. Geological Survey, Reston, Virginia: 2009

For more information on the USGS—the Federal source for science about the Earth, its natural and living resources, natural hazards, and the environment, visit http://www.usgs.gov or call 1-888-ASK-USGS.

For an overview of USGS information products, including maps, imagery, and publications, visit *http://www.usgs.gov/pubprod*

To order this and other USGS information products, visit *http://store.usgs.gov*

Suggested citation:
Eckhardt, D.A., Reddy, J.E., and Shaw, S.B., 2009, Groundwater quality in central New York, 2007: U.S. Geological Survey Open-File Report 2009-1257, 38 p., available online at http://pubs.usgs.gov/of/2009/1257.

Contents

Figures

Tables

Tables at end of report:

Conversion Factors, Abbreviations, and Datums

Multiply	By	To obtain
inch (in)	2.54	centimeter (mm)
foot (ft)	0.3048	meter (m)
square mile (mi^2)	2.590	square kilometer (km^2)
million gallons per day (Mgal/d)	0.04381	cubic meter per second (m^3/s)

Temperature in degrees Celsius (°C) may be converted to degrees Fahrenheit (°F) as follows:
°F=(1.8×°C)+32.

Abbreviations

AMCL	Alternative maximum contaminant level
CFU/mL	Colony forming units per milliliter
CIAT	2-Chloro-4-isopropylamino-6-amino-*s*-triazine (also called deethylatrazine)
CWS	Community water system
ESA	Ethanesulfonic acid
HA	Health Advisory for drinking water
HPC	Heterotrophic plate count
MCL	Maximum Contaminant Level
MTBE	Methyl *tert*-butyl ether
NWQL	USGS National Water Quality Laboratory
NYSDEC	New York State Department of Environmental Conservation
NYSDOH	New York State Department of Health
OA	Oxanilic acid
OGRL	USGS Organic Geochemistry Research Laboratory
OIET	2-Hydroxy-4-isopropylamino-6-ethylamino-*s*-triazine (also called hydroxyatrazine)
SMCL	Secondary Maximum Contaminant Level
USEPA	U.S. Environmental Protection Agency
USGS	U.S. Geological Survey
VOC	Volatile organic compound

Other abbreviations in this report
micrometer (μm)
micrograms per liter (μg/L)
milligrams per liter (mg/L)
microsiemens per centimeter (μS/cm)
platinum-cobalt units (Pt-Co units)
picocuries per liter (pCi/L)

Datums
Vertical coordinate information is referenced to the National Geodetic Vertical Datum of 1929 (NGVD 29).
Horizontal coordinate information is referenced to the North American Datum of 1983 (NAD 83).

Groundwater Quality in Central New York, 2007

By David A.V. Eckhardt, J.E. Reddy, and Stephen B. Shaw

Abstract

Water samples were collected from 7 production wells and 28 private residential wells in central New York from August through December 2007 and analyzed to characterize the chemical quality of groundwater. Seventeen wells are screened in sand and gravel aquifers, and 18 are finished in bedrock aquifers. The wells were selected to represent areas of greatest groundwater use and to provide a geographical sampling from the 5,799-square-mile study area. Samples were analyzed for 6 physical properties and 216 constituents, including nutrients, major inorganic ions, trace elements, radionuclides, pesticides, volatile organic compounds, phenolic compounds, organic carbon, and 4 types of bacteria.

Results indicate that groundwater used for drinking supply is generally of acceptable quality, although concentrations of some constituents or bacteria exceeded at least one drinking-water standard at several wells. The cations detected in the highest concentrations were calcium, magnesium, and sodium; anions detected in the highest concentrations were bicarbonate, chloride, and sulfate. The predominant nutrients were nitrate and ammonia, but no nutrients exceeded Maximum Contaminant Levels (MCLs). The trace elements barium, boron, lithium, and strontium were detected in every sample; the trace elements present in the highest concentrations were barium, boron, iron, lithium, manganese, and strontium. Fifteen pesticides, including seven pesticide degradates, were detected in water from 17 of the 35 wells, but none of the concentrations exceeded State or Federal MCLs. Sixteen volatile organic compounds were detected in water from 15 of the 35 wells.

Nine analytes and three types of bacteria were detected in concentrations that exceeded Federal and State drinking-water standards, which typically are identical. One sample had a water color that exceeded the U.S. Environmental Protection Agency (USEPA) Secondary Maximum Contaminant Level (SMCL) and the New York State MCL of 10 color units. Sulfate concentrations exceeded the USEPA SMCL and the New York State MCL of 250 milligrams per liter (mg/L) in two samples, and chloride concentrations exceeded the USEPA SMCL and the New York State MCL of 250 mg/L in two samples. Sodium concentrations exceeded the USEPA Drinking Water Health Advisory of 60 mg/L in eight samples. Iron concentrations exceeded the USEPA SMCL and the New York State MCL of 300 micrograms per liter (μg/L) in 10 filtered samples. Manganese exceeded the USEPA SMCL of 50 μg/L in 10 filtered samples and the New York State MCL of 300 μg/L in 1 filtered sample. Barium exceeded the MCL of 2,000 μg/L in one sample, and aluminum exceeded the SMCL of 50 μg/L in three samples. Radon-222 exceeded the proposed USEPA MCL of 300 picocuries per liter in 12 samples. One sample from a private residential well had a trichloroethene concentration of 50.8 μg/L, which exceeded the MCL of 5 μg/L. Any detection of coliform bacteria indicates a potential violation of New York State health regulations; total coliform bacteria were detected in 19 samples, and fecal coliform bacteria were detected in one sample. The plate counts for heterotrophic bacteria exceeded the MCL (500 colony-forming units per milliliter) in three samples.

Introduction

Water samples were collected from 7 production wells and 28 private residential wells in 18 counties in central New York from August through December 2007 and analyzed to characterize the chemical quality of groundwater in the 5,799-mi^2 study area. Thirty-one wells are within the Oswego River Basin (which contains the Seneca and Oneida River Basins), and four are in the central Lake Ontario Basin, which drains the area between Oswego and Rochester (fig. 1). Seventeen of the wells are screened in sand and gravel aquifers, and 18 are completed in bedrock aquifers.

Many studies of groundwater quality in New York have included parts of the study area, such as Weist and Geist (1969), Kantrowitz (1970), Crain (1975), Cartwright and Ziarno (1980), Waller and Finch (1982), Cosner (1984), and Yager and others (2007). These studies provide much useful information, but a more comprehensive and current assessment of the groundwater quality throughout the entire area is needed.

Section 305(b) of the Federal Clean Water Act Amendments of 1977 (U.S. Environmental Protection Agency, 1997) requires all States to implement a comprehensive water-quality-monitoring program for surface-water and groundwater resources. In 2001, the U.S. Geological Survey (USGS), in cooperation with the New York State Department of Environmental Conservation (NYSDEC) and the U.S. Environmental Protection Agency (USEPA), began an assessment of groundwater quality in major river basins throughout the State, as specified in Section 305(b). To date (2008), groundwater-quality studies have been completed in the Chemung River Basin (Hetcher-Aguila, 2004), the Lake Champlain Basin (Nystrom, 2006), the upper Susquehanna River Basin (Hetcher-Aguila and Eckhardt, 2006), the Delaware River Basin (Nystrom, 2007a), the St. Lawrence River Basin (Nystrom, 2007b), the Genesee River Basin (Eckhardt and others, 2007), the Mohawk River Basin (Nystrom, 2008), and three drainage basins in western New York (Eckhardt and others, 2008). In 2007, a study of groundwater quality in tributary basins that drain to Lake Ontario in central New York was completed and is the subject of this report.

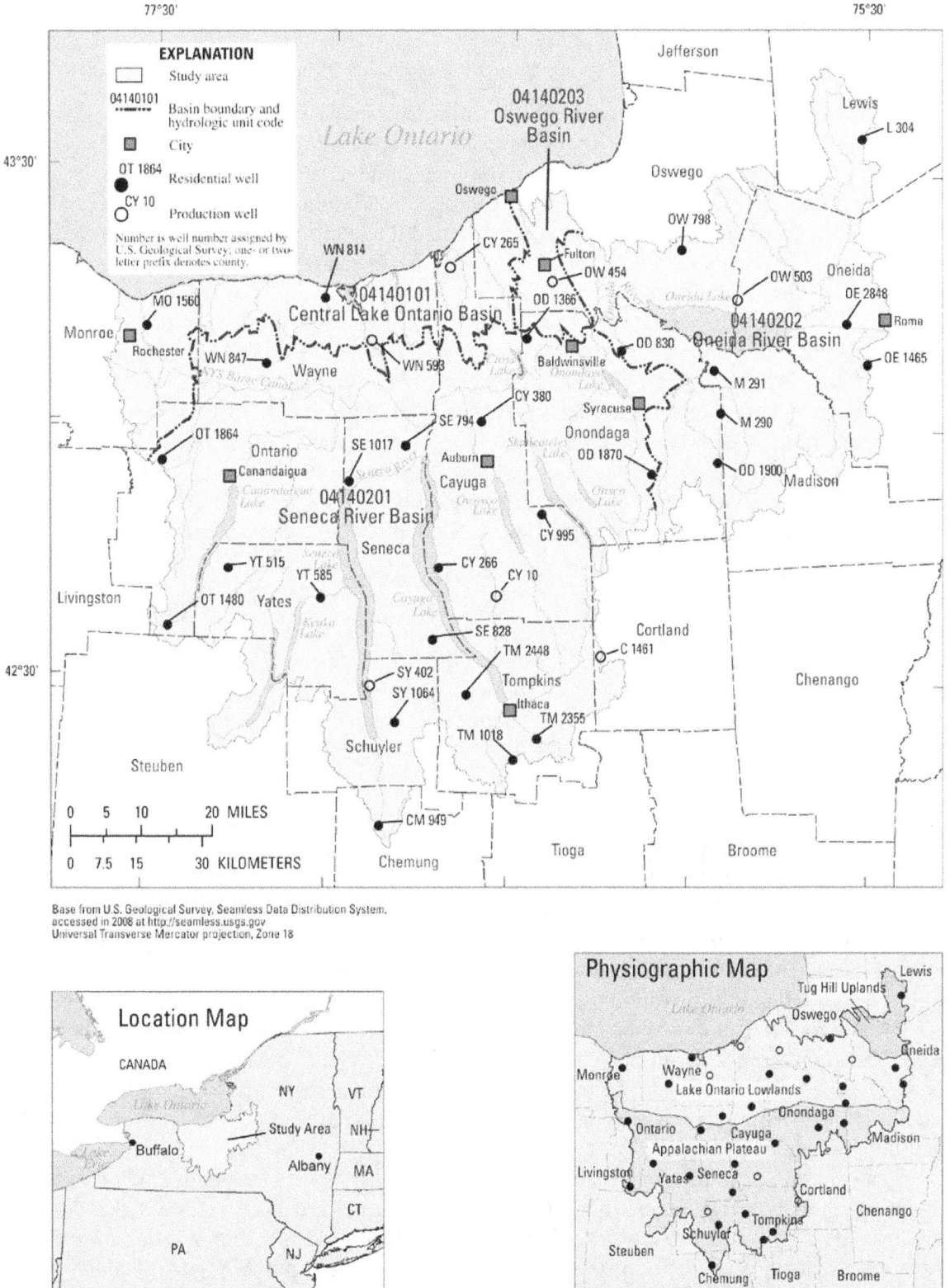

Figure 1. Pertinent geographic features of study area in central New York, and locations of the 35 wells sampled in 2007. (Well data are given in table A1 at end of report.)

Purpose and Scope

This report presents the results of the 2007 study of groundwater quality in central New York. It first describes the study area and the sampling methods, then presents results of the water-quality analyses. The area and population is given for each basin (table 1), and the land use, surficial geology, and bedrock geology is illustrated for the study area (figures 2 through 4). Summary statistics (number of samples exceeding Federal or State drinking-water standards) and the minimum, median, and maximum concentrations of all analytes in 35 samples from wells in sand and gravel and bedrock aquifers are given in tables 2-4; detailed analytical results are given in tables A1-A9 (at end of report). Analytical results for selected constituents are compared with Federal and New York State drinking-water standards, which are typically identical. The standards include Maximum Contaminant Levels (MCLs), Secondary Maximum Contaminant Levels (SMCLs), and Health Advisories (HAs) established by the USEPA (2002, 2004, and 2006) and the New York State Department of Health (NYSDOH, 2007b). MCLs specify the highest level of a contaminant that is allowed in drinking water; they are based on human health criteria and are legally enforceable by Federal and State authorities. SMCLs are non-enforceable guidelines based on cosmetic and aesthetic criteria, such as taste and odor. HAs are estimates of acceptable drinking-water levels for contaminants that can affect human health; they are non-enforceable standards that provide technical guidance for water use.

Study Area

The study area includes all or parts of 18 counties in north-central New York (fig. 1; table 1). It encompasses the central Lake Ontario Basin (between Oswego and Rochester) and the Oswego River Basin, which includes the Seneca River and Oneida River Basins and contains Oneida Lake, Onondaga Lake, and the seven easternmost Finger Lakes.

Physiography, Land Use, and Precipitation

The central and southern parts of the study area lie within the Appalachian Plateau physiographic province (fig. 1, table A1); the northern part lies in the Lake Ontario Lowlands and the Tug Hill Uplands. Forest and pasture dominate the upland rolling hills and narrow valleys of the southern and eastern parts of the study area. The central region has several deep and wide glacial valleys that drain northward and contain the Finger Lakes. Cultivation of row crops, apples, and grapes is common in the Lake Ontario Lowlands, and row-crop, forage-crop, and dairy farming are concentrated in the fertile soils that overlie carbonate bedrock areas between Buffalo and Albany (fig. 2). The Syracuse and Rochester metropolitan areas lie near the central and northwestern parts of the study area, respectively, and the New York State Barge Canal (formerly known as the Erie Canal) traverses the area from Rochester to Rome and from Syracuse to Oswego (fig. 1).

Land-surface elevations range from about 250 ft at Lake Ontario to about 2,000 ft in the western and southern uplands. The climate is humid, and air temperatures are moderated by Lake Ontario and the Finger Lakes. Virtually all groundwater in the area originates as precipitation, which ranges from about 32 inches per year (in/yr) in the south-central areas to about 52 in/yr in the Tug Hill Upland (fig. 1); mean annual precipitation is about 39 in. About 20 percent of the annual precipitation infiltrates the land surface and recharges the sand and gravel and bedrock aquifers (Randall, 2001).

4

Table 1. Basin areas and population of the central New York study area, by drainage basin.

[Basin locations are shown in figure 1. Population: 2000 Census (U.S. Department of Commerce, 2000)]

Drainage basin	Hydrologic unit code	Area (square miles)	Population
Oswego River [1]	04140201, 04140202, 041402033	5,097	1,043,194
Central Lake Ontario [2]	04140101	702	548,940

[1] Includes the Seneca River and Oneida River basins.

[2] Includes tributary basins to Lake Ontario between the Oswego River and the Genesee River basins.

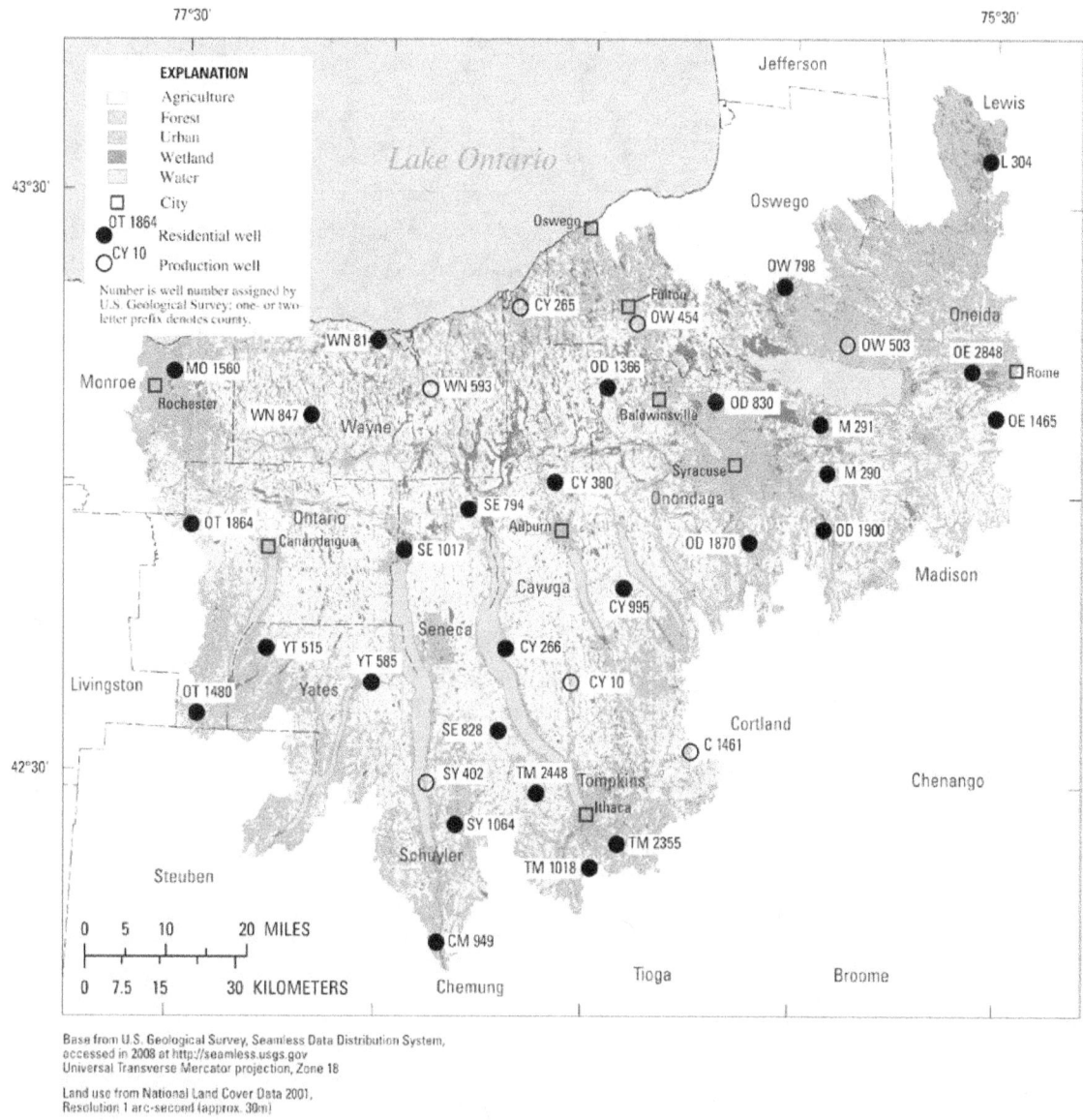

Figure 2. Land use in central New York study area and locations of the 35 wells sampled in 2007. (Well data are given in table A1.)

Glacial Deposits

Glacially derived deposits are generally present throughout central New York (fig. 3). Glaciers scoured the hills and valleys of New York and left a thin mantle of till on top of the bedrock in upland areas and morainal deposits of fine-grained, poorly sorted material that formed valley plugs and low ridges (Cadwell and Muller, 1986). During the subsequent period of deglaciation, meltwater streams deposited thick layers of stratified drift (glaciofluvial sand and gravel) in front of the glaciers and on top, beneath, and alongside them to form deposits that are present as outwash plains, eskers, kettles, kames, and kame terraces. In some areas near Lake Ontario, thick sequences of beach sands were deposited along the shores of proglacial lakes. These water-borne deposits of sand and gravel, where saturated with groundwater, now form locally significant aquifers. Glacial meltwaters also deposited fine particles in proglacial lakes, where they settled to form poorly permeable deposits of lacustrine clay, silt, and fine sand. Recent alluvial deposits cover some of the glacial deposits and form floodplains along the larger streams and rivers and on the terraces along the shore of Lake Ontario. The glacial deposits within the study area are described in detail by Fairchild (1928), Coates (1966), Waller and Finch (1982), Miller (1982, 1988, 1990), Randall (2001), and Kontis and others (2004).

Bedrock

The bedrock aquifers in the study area (fig. 4) consist of relatively flat-lying, interbedded sedimentary units of shale, siltstone, sandstone, limestone, and dolostone of Ordovician, Silurian, and Devonian age (Broughton and others, 1962; Isachsen and others, 2000). Two bands of carbonate-rock aquifers—limestones and dolostones—extend from Rochester to Rome, and from Canandaigua to east of Syracuse; interbedded Silurian shale, dolostone, and evaporites (salt and gypsum) crop out in the area between the carbonate-rock aquifers.

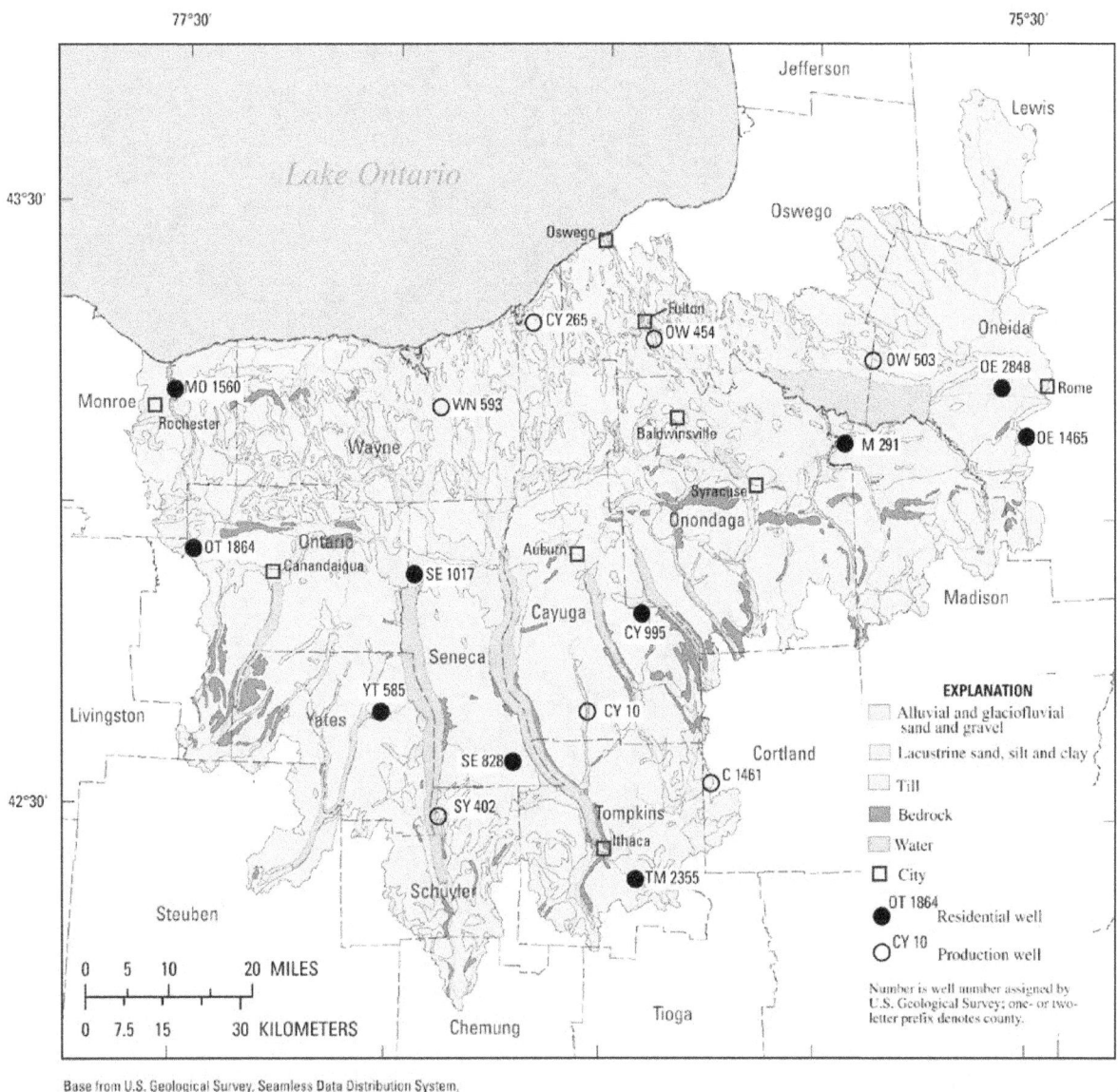

Figure 3. Generalized surficial geology of central New York study area and locations of the 17 wells screened in sand and gravel aquifers that were sampled in 2007. (Well data are given in table A1.)

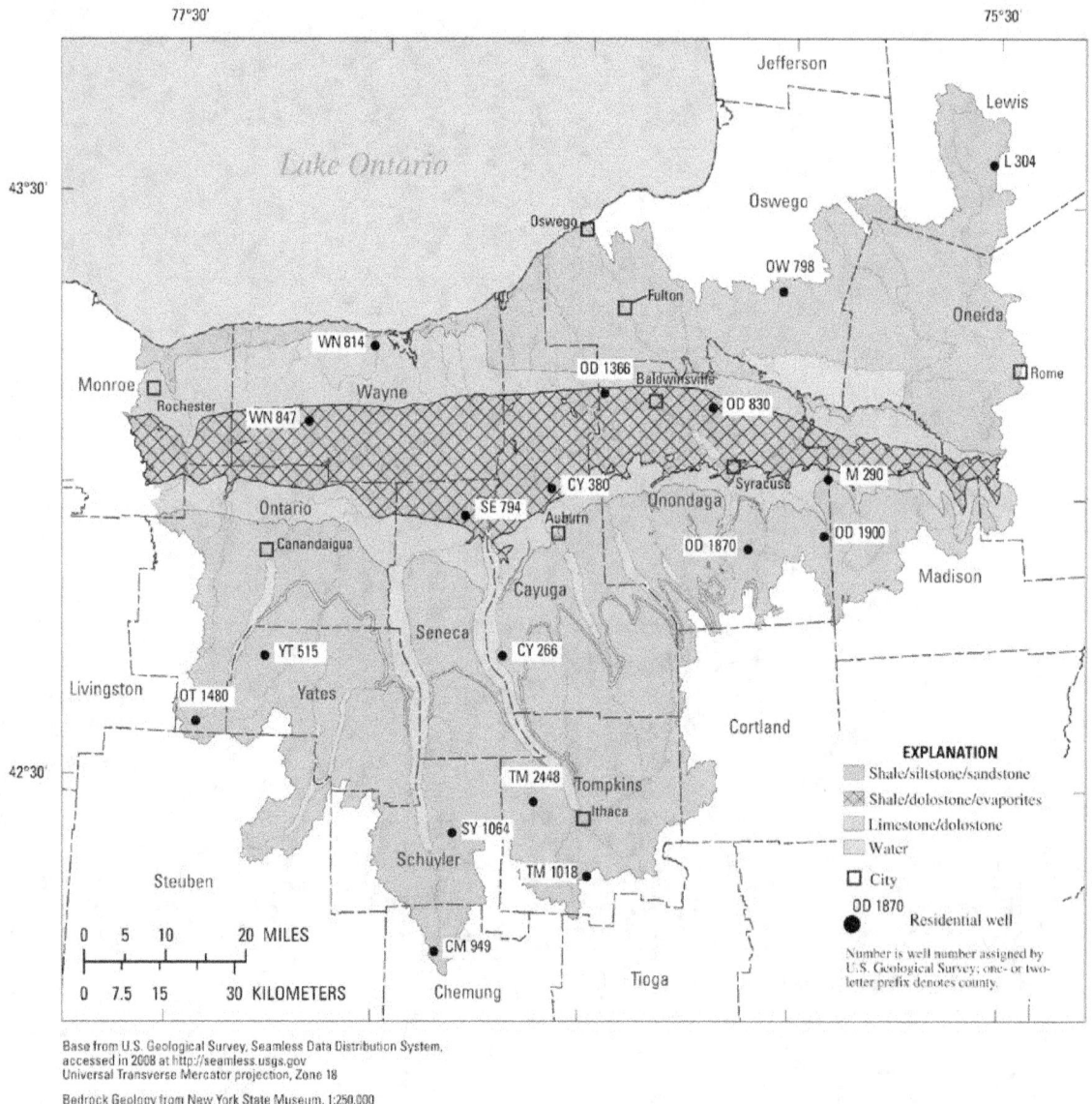

Figure 4. Generalized bedrock geology of central New York study area and locations of the 18 wells completed in bedrock that were sampled in 2007. (Well data are given in table A1.)

Population and Water Supply

Most of the study area is predominantly rural, but it includes the large cities of Syracuse and Rochester and several small cities such as Auburn, Fulton, Ithaca, Oswego, Rome, and many villages and hamlets (fig. 1). The largest developed, urban areas are Syracuse and Rochester and their suburbs in Onondaga and Monroe Counties (fig. 2). Total population of the study area in 2000 was about 1.6 million, about half of which lives in the Syracuse and Rochester metropolitan areas (U.S. Department of Commerce, 2000). Production wells (wells that provide water for more than 25 people) supply about 35 million gallons per day (Mgal/d) of water for commercial and domestic use within the study area (New York State Department of Health, 2007a).

The largest water suppliers are the Onondaga County Water Authority, which provides the residents of the Syracuse area with water from Skaneateles and Otisco Lakes and Lake Ontario, and the Monroe County Water Authority, which provides residents in the Rochester area with water from Lake Ontario. Many small cities such as Ithaca and Auburn tap reservoirs and lakes for their water supply, but many rural communities that lie in areas beyond municipal water-supply lines rely on community water-system (production) wells that tap groundwater from bedrock or from surficial deposits of sand and gravel. Most homeowners that live in rural areas have private wells that tap local surficial deposits or bedrock.

The most productive aquifers within the study area are the glacial and alluvial deposits of sand and gravel (fig. 3). Anderson and others (1982) estimated that sand and gravel aquifers near Fulton can yield as much as 250 gallons per minute (gal/min). Some wells completed in the sand and gravel aquifer adjacent to the Oswego River may induce surface-water infiltration. Wells in the sand and gravel deposits along the Seneca River south and east of Baldwinsville may potentially yield more than 350 gal/min (Kantrowitz, 1970; Pagano and others, 1986). Till deposits cover much of the upland areas, but they are typically thin, relatively impermeable, and yield little water to wells. Lacustrine fine sand, silt, and clay deposits are present in most large valleys but yield little or no water to wells. The fine-grained beds confine and help protect productive sand and gravel aquifers that lie beneath them. Bedrock aquifers (fig. 4) are used for water supply where sand and gravel aquifers are absent, typically in upland areas. The bedrock aquifers in the study area may yield water of poorer chemical quality than the surficial aquifers; for example, the carbonate rock aquifers typically yield very hard water, and shale bedrock aquifers near Onondaga Lake and Lake Ontario may yield salty water (Kantrowitz, 1970; Crain, 1975; Yager and others, 2007).

Methods

A total of 35 wells were selected for sample collection—17 are finished in sand and gravel aquifers (fig. 3), and 18 are finished in bedrock aquifers (fig. 4). Of the 17 wells that tap sand and gravel aquifers, 7 are production wells and 10 are private residential wells. All of the 18 bedrock wells are private residential wells. Sampling was done from August through December 2007. The water samples were analyzed for 6 physical properties and 216 constituents, including 4 types of bacteria. Three samples—two field blanks and one replicate sample—were collected for quality assurance (QA) and quality control (QC), as required for the Federal 305(b) program.

Site Selection

Wells were selected to provide a spatial representation of water use within the study area. The wells were identified through (1) the USGS National Water Information System (NWIS) database, (2) the NYSDEC Water-Well Reporting Program, and (3) information from State and county health departments. The Water-Well Reporting Program was implemented in 2000 to collect information on well construction, geology, and yield for newly drilled wells throughout New York from licensed well drillers; the resulting database provides useful information for groundwater studies. A letter requesting permission to sample the water was sent to owners of residential wells that were identified as potential sampling sites; the letter described the project and included a questionnaire requesting information on the location of the well, the most convenient times for sampling, any safety concerns around the well, and other information.

Production wells were identified through the NYSDOH and by local water managers of villages and cities throughout the study area. The water managers were sent a project description and a questionnaire similar to those sent to residential well owners. Residential and production well owners who responded favorably were contacted by telephone to clarify information about the wells and to arrange sampling dates.

Most of the wells finished in sand and gravel aquifers (fig. 3) are in valleys, and the well depths ranged from 31 to 145 ft (table A1). All the production wells that tap sand and gravel aquifers have slotted screens, whereas most residential wells that tap sand and gravel simply have an open-ended steel casing. The bedrock wells (fig. 4) are generally in upland terrains, and depths ranged from 33 to 300 ft (table A1); these wells typically have a steel casing set into open boreholes in competent rock, and water yields are obtained by flow through bedrock fractures to the well.

Site selection did not target specific municipality, industrial, or agricultural practices; rather, sampling sites were selected to represent areas of greatest groundwater use and to obtain a geographical representation of the study area and its aquifers (figs. 2-4). Site selection included wells in each of four predominant land-use categories—agriculture, urban, forest, and wetland.

Shallow wells that tap sand and gravel aquifers are susceptible to contamination by several types of compounds, including volatile organic compounds (VOCs), pesticides, deicing chemicals, and nutrients from nearby highways and industrial, agricultural, and residential areas. The movement of these contaminants to the water table through the soils and surficial sand and gravel can be relatively rapid. Bedrock wells that tap sandstone and shale aquifers in rural upland areas are generally less susceptible to contamination from industrial and urban sources, which are mainly in the valleys; but bedrock wells in lowland areas underlain by carbonate rock (limestone and dolostone) may be vulnerable to contamination from surface runoff because infiltration rates and groundwater flow can be relatively rapid through solution features in the rock. Agricultural land that surrounds wells may be a potential source of contamination from fertilizers, pesticides, and fecal waste from livestock; lawns and residential septic systems also are a potential source of these contaminants. In addition to contaminants from human activities, the aquifers contain naturally derived elements that may diminish water quality, such as sodium, chloride, sulfate, iron, manganese, and trace elements such as arsenic; some aquifers may contain hydrogen sulfide, methane, and radon gases from deep-lying sources.

Sampling Methods

Water samples were analyzed for the physical properties and constituents listed in Appendix tables A2-A9 (at end of report). The categories are as follows: physical properties (table A3), inorganic constituents (table A4), nutrients and total organic carbon (table A5), trace elements and radon-222 (table A6), pesticides (table A7), VOCs (table A8), bacterial water-quality indicators (table A9), and phenols (none detected, table A2). Samples were collected from every well for these analyses and were processed by methods described in USGS manuals for the collection of water-quality data (U.S. Geological Survey, variously dated). Samples collected for pesticide analyses were processed by the methods of Shelton (1994), Sandstrom and others (2001), and Wilde and others (2004). These samples were analyzed at the USGS National Water Quality Laboratory (NWQL) and the USGS Kansas Organic Geochemistry Research Laboratory (OGRL) for 132 pesticides and pesticide degradates through methods described by Zaugg and others (1995), Furlong and others (2001), Sandstrom and others (2001), Meyer and others (1993), and Lee and Strahan (2003). The analytical method devised by Zaugg and others (1995) was developed in cooperation with the USEPA and allows detection of the Nation's most commonly used pesticides. Samples for bacterial analyses were processed in accordance with NYSDOH guidelines.

Sampling was done at all sites in the following steps. The well pump was turned on (many of the production wells were already running) and allowed to run until at least five casing volumes of well water had passed the sampling point. A raw-water tap between the well and the pressure tank was opened, and the water was allowed to flush for several minutes. During this time, a visual evaluation of the area surrounding the well was conducted to identify potential sources of contamination that could affect the well water. Samples were collected from the raw-water tap to avoid all water-treatment systems and to ensure that the water collected was representative of the aquifer. A Teflon® discharge line was then connected to the tap, and samples were analyzed with a multiprobe meter for physical properties (temperature, specific conductance, dissolved-oxygen concentration, and pH). After the measurements of these properties had stabilized, a second Teflon® discharge line was connected to the first with a stainless-steel quick-connect fitting and was directed into a sample-collection chamber mounted on a plastic box; this chamber was used to minimize sample exposure to dust and other potential sources of contamination. Bottles were filled within the chamber according to standard USGS field methods (U.S. Geological Survey, 2007).

The analyses for physical properties, most trace elements and metals, acid-neutralizing capacity, organic carbon, radon-222, VOCs, and phenols were done on unfiltered water samples to obtain total whole-water concentrations. Dissolved concentrations of nutrients, major inorganic constituents, three metals, and pesticides were obtained from filtered samples. Concentrations of iron and manganese in unfiltered samples were compared with those in filtered samples to obtain the difference between the total and dissolved concentrations (table A6). To prevent sample degradation, sulfuric acid was added to the samples collected for phenol analysis, hydrochloric acid was added to samples collected for total organic carbon and VOC analyses, and nitric acid was added to some of the samples collected for trace-element analyses. Samples collected for analysis of dissolved inorganic compounds were filtered through a 0.45-micrometer (µm) cellulose capsule filter that was attached to the Teflon® discharge line inside the sample-collection chamber; samples for analysis of pesticides were filtered through a 0.7-µm furnace-baked glass-fiber plate filter using the methods of Wilde and others (2004).

All Teflon® discharge lines were cleaned in the laboratory before each sampling day and in the field between each sample collection. New sample-chamber bags were used at each sampling site. Samples for radon analysis were obtained through an in-line septum chamber with a disposable syringe to avoid atmospheric contamination. Samples for bacterial analysis were collected in sterile containers provided by the bacteriological laboratory; the connection of the sampling tube to the well tap was not sterilized.

The samples were stored on ice in coolers and delivered directly, or shipped by overnight delivery, to the following four laboratories: (1) the USGS NWQL in Denver, Colorado, for analysis for inorganic major ions, nutrients, inorganic trace elements and radon-222, some pesticides, and VOCs; (2) the USGS OGRL in Lawrence, Kansas, for other pesticides; (3) a New York State-certified private laboratory in Melville, NY, for total organic carbon and phenolic compounds; and (4) a laboratory in Ithaca, NY, approved by New York State for bacterial analysis.

Groundwater Quality

The 35 groundwater samples collected during this study were analyzed for 6 physical properties and 216 constituents, including 4 types of bacteria. Most (137) of the chemical constituents were not detected in any sample (table A2). The results of the physical-property measurements are listed in table A3. The concentrations of the 75 detected chemical constituents are listed in tables A4-A8, and the results for 4 types of bacteria are listed in table A9. The quality of the sampled groundwater was generally within NYSDOH and USEPA guidelines, although in some samples the concentrations of certain constituents exceeded recommended MCLs, SMCLs, or HAs set by the USEPA (2006) and the NYSDOH (2007b). In general, most of the water-quality problems involve taste or odor and excessive hardness, iron, or manganese that develop from natural interactions of water and rock minerals in the subsurface.

11

The QA/QC field blanks contained no constituent in concentrations greater than the laboratory reporting levels, except toluene, which was detected in one blank sample at a trace concentration of 0.1 µg/L; this indicates that little to no contamination occurred through the sampling or analytical procedures. The results of analysis of the two QA/QC replicate samples indicate that variability in sample results meet the precision requirements of the study. The analytes with the largest percent differences between concentration in a groundwater sample and that in the replicate sample were acid-neutralizing capacity, residue on evaporation, and low-concentration trace elements (concentrations near the laboratory reporting level for the elements).

Physical Properties

The pH of the samples (table A3) ranged from 6.8 to 8.3, and none of the 35 samples was outside the accepted SMCL range of 6.5 to 8.5 (U.S. Environmental Protection Agency, 2006). Specific conductance of the samples ranged from 141 to 11,700 µS/cm. Dissolved oxygen concentrations ranged from less than 0.3 mg/L (the analytical detection limit) at 10 wells to 9.1 mg/L at one well. One sample had a water color that exceeded the Federal SMCL and the New York State MCL of 15 platinum-cobalt units. The odor of hydrogen sulfide gas, which may occur in the absence of oxygen, was noted by field personnel in water from 8 of the 35 wells.

Inorganic Major Ions

Water from the wells was generally a calcium-bicarbonate type, although water from two wells [MO 1560 and TM 1018] (fig. 1) was a sodium-bicarbonate type. Water from two wells [OE 1465 and YT 515] was a sodium-chloride type, and water from one well [SE 794] was a calcium-sulfate type (Hem, 1985). The cations that were detected in the highest concentrations were calcium, magnesium, and sodium (tables 2 and A4). Calcium concentrations ranged from 15.0 to 489 mg/L, and magnesium concentrations ranged from 5.46 to 115 mg/L. Calcium and magnesium contribute to water hardness, and 22 of the 35 wells yielded water with hardness greater than 180 mg/L, which is classified as "very hard" (Hem, 1985). The median hardness is 260 mg/L for samples from sand and gravel wells and 175 mg/L for samples from bedrock wells. Sodium concentrations ranged from 1.20 to 1,870 mg/L, and the USEPA Health Advisory (HA), which recommends that sodium concentrations in drinking water not exceed 60 mg/L to minimize the taste, was exceeded in eight samples. This HA for sodium is not federally enforceable but is intended as a guideline for consumers (U.S. Environmental Protection Agency, 2002, 2006).

The anions that were detected in the highest concentrations were bicarbonate (alkalinity), chloride, and sulfate (tables 2 and A4). Bicarbonate concentrations ranged from 78 to 742 mg/L (as $CaCO_3$). Chloride concentrations ranged from 0.68 to 3,380 mg/L; the Federal SMCL and the New York State MCL of 250 mg/L for chloride was exceeded in two samples. Sulfate concentrations ranged from less than 0.18 mg/L (the analytical detection limit) to 543 mg/L; the Federal SMCL and the New York State MCL of 250 mg/L for sulfate was exceeded in two samples.

Table 2. Summary statistics for concentrations of major ions in sand and gravel aquifers and bedrock aquifers in central New York, 2007.

[Concentrations are in milligrams per liter (mg/L). All samples represent filtered water; –, not applicable; <, less than; E, estimated]

Constituent		Drinking-water standard	Number of samples exceeding standard	Sand and gravel (17 samples)			Bedrock (18 samples)		
				Mini-mum	Median	Maxi-mum	Mini-mum	Median	Maxi-mum
Cations	Calcium	–	–	18.2	73.1	132	15.0	50.6	489
	Magnesium	–	–	5.46	22.3	47.8	7.64	14.4	115
	Potassium	–	–	.41	1.31	5.62	.65	1.97	37.7
	Sodium	[1]60	8	1.20	14.2	343	2.14	24.2	1,870
Anions	Bicarbonate	–	–	78	322	445	101	250	742
	Chloride	[2,3]250	2	1.49	26.7	663	.68	16.6	3,380
	Fluoride	[2]2.2, [3]2.0	0	< .12	.11	.42	E .07	.19	.92
	Sulfate	[2,3]250	2	< .18	26.1	139	E .14	26.9	543
Hardness, mg/L as CaCO$_3$				68	260	490	84	175	1,700
Alkalinity, mg/L as CaCO$_3$				64	263	365	83	211	608
Residue on evaporation, mg/L				74	348	1,400	98	328	7,130

[1] USEPA Drinking Water Health Advisory (taste threshold).

[2] NYSDOH Maximum Contaminant Level.

[3] USEPA Secondary Maximum Contaminant Level.

Nutrients and Organic Carbon

Nitrate and ammonia were the predominant nutrients in the groundwater samples (tables 3 and A5); nitrite and organic nitrogen concentrations were negligible in most samples. Nitrate plus nitrite concentrations ranged from less than 0.04 (the analytical detection limit) to 7.34 mg/L as nitrogen (N); the median concentration was 0.25 mg/L in samples from sand and gravel wells and 0.07 mg/L in samples from bedrock wells. The nitrate MCL of 10 mg/L (as N) was not exceeded in any sample, and the concentrations in 17 of the 35 samples were below the detection limit. Ammonia concentrations ranged from less than 0.02 to 4.33 mg/L as N. Orthophosphate was detected in 34 of the 35 samples, but concentrations were low; the maximum concentration was 0.047 mg/L (as phosphorus). Total organic carbon was detected in 16 of the 35 samples; concentrations ranged from less than 1.0 mg/L (the analytical detection limit) to 2.7 mg/L.

Table 3. Summary statistics for concentrations of nutrients and organic carbon in sand and gravel aquifers and bedrock aquifers in central New York, 2007.

[All samples represent filtered water except as noted; mg/L, milligrams per liter; –, not applicable; <, less than; E, estimated; N, nitrogen; P, phosphorus]

Constituent	Drinking-water standard	Number of samples exceeding standard	Sand and gravel (17 samples)			Bedrock (18 samples)		
			Minimum	Median	Maximum	Minimum	Median	Maximum
Ammonia plus organic N, mg/L as N	–	–	< 0.10	E 0.06	0.37	< 0.10	0.17	4.5
Ammonia, mg/L as N	–	–	< 0.020	E .020	.335	< 0.020	.110	4.33
Nitrate plus nitrite, mg/L as N	[1,2]10	0	< .04	.25	7.34	< .04	.07	5.35
Nitrite, mg/L as N	[1,2]1	0	< .002	< .002	.089	< .002	< .002	.039
Orthophosphate, mg/L as P	–	–	E .003	E .005	.031	< .006	E .005	.047
Total organic carbon, unfiltered, mg/L	–	–	< 1.0	1.1	2.4	< 1.0	< 1.0	2.7

[1] USEPA Maximum Contaminant Level.

[2] NYSDOH Maximum Contaminant Level.

Trace Elements and Radon-222

The trace elements most commonly detected in the 35 samples were barium, boron, lithium, and strontium, all of which were detected in every sample (tables 4 and A6). The elements detected in the highest concentrations were barium, boron, iron, lithium, manganese, and strontium. Barium concentrations ranged from 10.5 to 10,400 µg/L, and the MCL for barium (2,000 µg/L) was exceeded once. Boron concentrations ranged from 5.0 to 3,140 µg/L; MCLs have not been established for boron. Iron was detected in 26 of the 35 filtered samples at concentrations ranging from 4 to 3,530 µg/L (table A6); the Federal SMCL and the New York State MCL for iron (300 µg/L) was exceeded in 10 samples. Lithium concentrations ranged from 1.3 to 1,900 µg/L; MCLs have not been established for lithium. Manganese was detected in 31 of the 35 filtered samples at concentrations ranging from 0.2 µg/L to 515 µg/L; the Federal SMCL for manganese (50 µg/L) was exceeded in 10 filtered samples, and the New York State MCL (300 µg/L) was exceeded in one filtered sample. Strontium concentrations ranged from 32.9 to 53,800 µg/L, but MCLs have not been established for strontium.

Aluminum was detected in 24 of the 35 samples, and the SMCL (50 µg/L) was exceeded in samples from three wells. Arsenic was detected in 24 samples, but the MCL (10 µg/L) was not exceeded. Lead was detected in 34 samples, but the MCL (15 µg/L) was not exceeded.

Uranium was detected in 30 samples, but none exceeded the MCL of 30 µg/L. The MCLs for antimony (6 µg/L), beryllium (4 µg/L), cadmium (5 µg/L), chromium (100 µg/L), selenium (50 µg/L), and silver (100 µg/L) and the SMCLs for copper (1,000 µg/L) and zinc (5,000 µg/L) were not exceeded in any sample. Mercury was not detected in any sample (table A2).

Radon-222 was detected in every sample (table A6), and concentrations ranged from 70 to 1,000 pCi/L. The median concentration was 170 pCi/L in samples from sand and gravel wells and 215 pCi/L in samples from bedrock wells. The proposed MCL of 300 pCi/L for radon-222 in drinking water was exceeded in 12 samples, but the proposed Alternate Maximum Contaminant Level AMCL of 4,000 pCi/L was not exceeded. The AMCL is the proposed allowable concentration of radon in raw-water samples where the State has implemented mitigation programs to address the health risks of radon in indoor air. The proposed MCL and AMCL for radon are under review and have not been adopted (U.S. Environmental Protection Agency, 2004, 2006).

Table 4. Summary statistics for concentrations of trace elements and radon-222 in sand and gravel aquifers and bedrock aquifers in central New York, 2007.

[All concentrations are in micrograms per liter (µg/L) except as noted. All samples unfiltered except as noted. pCi/L, picocuries per liter; –, not applicable; E, estimated; <, less than]

Constituent	Drinking-water standard	Number of samples exceeding standard	Sand and gravel (17 samples)			Bedrock (18 samples)		
			Minimum	Median	Maximum	Minimum	Median	Maximum
Aluminum	[3]50	3	< 2	E 2	41	< 4	9	4,830
Antimony	[1,2]6	0	< .1	< .2	.2	< .1	<.2	.5
Arsenic	[1]10	0	< .60	E .12	7.2	< .60	.39	8.7
Barium	[1,2]2,000	1	10.5	66.7	630	12.3	108	10,400
Beryllium	[1,2]4	0	< .04	< .06	< .08	< .04	< .04	.20
Boron, filtered	–	–	6.0	21	111	5.0	113	3,140
Cadmium	[1,2]5	0	< .01	< 0.02	.06	< .01	< 0.02	.02
Chromium	[1,2]100	0	< .04	< .60	E .48	< .40	< .60	44.4
Cobalt	–	–	< .04	E .02	.17	< .04	.04	4.70
Copper	[3]1,000	0	< 1.2	1.3	14	< 1.2	1.6	180
Iron, filtered	[2,3]300	10	< 8	49	1,930	< 6	41	3,530
Iron	[2,3]300	14	< 6	158	2,860	< 6	174	9,190
Lead	[4]15	0	.06	.27	2.11	< .03	.33	4.00
Lithium	–	–	1.3	5.1	42.7	2.7	22.9	1,900
Manganese, filtered	[3]50 - [2]300	10 - 1	< .4	29.1	176	.3	8.5	515
Manganese	[3]50 - [2]300	12 - 2	< .4	32.9	178	1.1	18.0	594
Molybdenum	–	–	< .1	.5	3.5	.1	.5	6.0
Nickel	–	–	< .12	.18	1.5	< .12	.30	25.4
Selenium	[1,2]50	0	< .08	< .08	.21	< .08	< .08	5.9
Silver	[1,2]100	0	< 0.02	< 0.02	< .04	< 0.02	< 0.02	.06
Strontium	–	–	32.9	180	1,100	46.5	1,545	53,800
Thallium	–	–	< .08	< .18	E .05	< .08	< .08	< .40
Uranium	[1]30	0	< .012	.297	2.36	< .012	.206	28.3
Zinc	[2,3]5,000	0	< 2.0	2.9	23.1	< 2.0	5.8	74.9
Radon-222, pCi/L	[5]300	12	70	170	680	70	215	1,000

[1] USEPA Maximum Contaminant Level.

[2] NYSDOH Maximum Contaminant Level.

[3] USEPA Secondary Maximum Contaminant Level.

[4] USEPA Treatment Technique.

[5] USEPA Proposed Maximum Contaminant Level.

Pesticides

Fifteen pesticides (including 7 pesticide degradates) were detected in water from 17 of the 35 wells (table A7), but none of the concentrations exceeded MCLs. Ten of the samples containing pesticides were from sand and gravel aquifers, and seven were from bedrock aquifers. Caffeine, which is not a pesticide, is measured as part of the pesticide analyses and can be an indicator of human wastes, but it was not detected in any sample (table A2). The pesticide compounds that were detected most frequently were herbicide degradation products—CIAT (2-chloro-4-isopropylamino-6-amino-s-triazine, also called deethylatrazine, a degradation product of atrazine and propazine), alachlor ESA (a degradation product of alachlor), and metolachlor ESA and OA (degradation products of metolachlor). CIAT was detected in nine samples, alachlor ESA in seven samples, and metolachlor ESA and OA in four samples each. The maximum concentration of any herbicide degradation product was 1.51 µg/L (metolachlor ESA). Metolachlor was detected once (0.006 µg/L). Atrazine was detected in six samples; the maximum concentration was 0.088 µg/L. Alachlor was not detected (table A2), but its degradation products (alachlor ESA and alachlor ESA 2d amide) were present in eight samples. No Federal MCLs currently have been established for pesticide degradation products, and no pesticide concentration exceeded Federal or New York State MCLs. These trace-level detections of pesticides are similar to those reported by Eckhardt and others (2001), Phillips and others (1999), and Eckhardt and Stackelberg (1995) from studies of pesticides in groundwater throughout New York State.

Volatile Organic Compounds and Phenolic Compounds

Sixteen VOCs were detected in 15 samples (table A8); the concentration of one compound (trichloroethene) in a sample from one private residential well (50.8 µg/L at SE 794) exceeded the MCL of 5 µg/L. Phenolic compounds, which are semivolatile, were not detected in any sample (table A2). Toluene was detected in nine samples; the maximum concentration was 1.0 µg/L. Trichloromethane (chloroform) was detected in five samples, bromodichloromethane and dibromochloromethane were each detected in three samples, and tribromomethane was detected in one sample; these four compounds are called trihalomethanes and are typically formed as by-products when chlorine or bromine are used to disinfect water. New disinfection by-product regulations for primary (production well) water sources have been established (U.S. Environmental Protection Agency, 1998). The regulations specify a MCL goal of zero for bromodichloromethane. Of the three samples in which bromodichloromethane were detected, only one was from a production well (CY 10). Xylene compounds were detected in one sample; the maximum concentration was 1.4 µg/L for the *meta* plus *para* isomers. Methyl *tert*-butyl ether (MTBE), a gasoline additive that can infiltrate into groundwater from leaking fuel tanks, was not detected in any sample (table A2).

Bacteria

All samples were analyzed for total coliform, fecal coliform, *Escherichia coli (E. coli)*, and heterotrophic bacteria. Total coliform was detected in 19 samples, and fecal coliform was detected once. *E. coli* was not detected (table A9). The coliform bacteria were detected in 6 samples from sand and gravel aquifers and in 13 samples from bedrock aquifers; 18 of the samples were from private residential wells, and one was from a production well (WN 593; fig. 1), which taps a sand and gravel aquifer. The presence of these bacteria is considered a potential violation of New York State health regulations and would require confirmation of the bacterial detection in additional samples, which was beyond the scope of this study. Accordingly, well owners were notified of positive results upon receipt of laboratory results. The raw-water samples collected in this study were collected prior to disinfection treatments, and production wells that provide water supply have chlorination systems that eliminate potential contamination by bacteria before the water is distributed to consumers. However, private residential wells typically lack a chlorination system.

Heterotrophic plate counts (HPCs) ranged from less than 1 (absent) to 6,880 colony-forming units per milliliter (CFU/mL; table A9). The USEPA MCL for HPC is 500 CFU/mL, and three samples exceeded this limit.

Summary

In 2001, the USGS, in cooperation with the NYSDEC and the USEPA, began an assessment of groundwater quality in bedrock and sand and gravel aquifers throughout New York State. As a part of the assessment in central New York, water samples were collected from 7 production wells and 28 private residential wells from August through December 2007 and were analyzed for 6 physical properties and 216 constituents that include inorganic major ions, nutrients, total organic carbon, trace elements, radon-222, VOCs, phenolic compounds, pesticides, and bacteria. The quality of the sampled groundwater was generally acceptable, although in samples from 30 wells the concentrations of at least one constituent exceeded recommended MCLs, SMCLs, or HAs set by the USEPA and the NYSDOH. Of the 75 chemical constituents that were detected, 9 exceeded Federal and State MCLs, SMCLs, or HAs at specific wells, and 3 types of bacteria were detected in concentrations that exceeded MCLs at some wells.

The cations that were detected in the highest concentrations are calcium, magnesium, and sodium; the anions that are detected in the highest concentrations were bicarbonate, chloride, and sulfate. The predominant nutrients were nitrate and ammonia; no sample exceeded the MCL (10 mg/L as N) for nitrate. The Health Advisory for sodium in drinking water (60 mg/L) was exceeded in eight of the 35 samples. The Federal SMCL and the State MCL for sulfate (250 mg/L) were exceeded in two samples; and the Federal SMCL and State MCL for chloride (250 mg/L) were exceeded in two samples. The water color of one sample exceeded the Federal SMCL and the State MCL (10 color units).

The trace elements detected in the highest concentrations were barium, boron, iron, lithium, manganese, and strontium; for all trace elements, only barium, iron, manganese, and aluminum concentrations exceeded SMCLs. Barium was detected in all 35 samples, and the MCL (2,000 µg/L) was exceeded once. Iron was detected in 26 of the 35 filtered samples, and the Federal SMCL and State MCL for iron (300 µg/L) was exceeded in 10 samples. Manganese was detected in 31 filtered samples. The USEPA SMCL (50 µg/L) was exceeded in 10 filtered samples, and the State MCL (300 µg/L) was exceeded in 1 filtered sample. Aluminum was detected in 24 samples, and the SMCL (50 µg/L) was exceeded in three samples. Arsenic was detected in 24 samples, but the MCL for arsenic (10 µg/L) was not exceeded in any sample. Lead was detected in 34 samples, but the MCL (15 µg/L) was not exceeded. Radon-222 was detected in every sample. The proposed USEPA MCL for radon-222 in drinking water (300 pCi/L) was exceeded in 12 samples, but the proposed AMCL (4,000 pCi/L) was not exceeded in any sample.

Fifteen pesticides, including 7 pesticide degradates, were detected in water from 17 of the 35 wells. Most of the concentrations were at or near the detection limits, and no concentration exceeded an MCL. Ten of the samples containing pesticides were from sand and gravel aquifers, and seven were from bedrock aquifers. Sixteen VOCs were detected in 15 samples, and one trichloroethene concentration (50.8 µg/L) exceeded the MCL of 5 µg/L at a private residential well. The presence of total coliform or fecal coliform bacteria is considered a potential violation of New York State MCLs. In this study, total coliform was detected in 19 samples, fecal coliform was detected once, and E. coli was not detected. Heterotrophic plate counts exceeded the MCL of 500 CFU/mL in three samples.

References Cited

Anderson, H.R., Stelz, W.G., Mier, J.B., Miller, T.S., Allen, R.V., and Muller, E.H., 1982, Geohydrology of the glaciolacustrine aquifer in the Fulton area, Oswego County, New York: U.S. Geological Survey Open-File Report 82–83, 7 sheets, scale 1:24,000.

Broughton, J.G., Fisher, D.W., Isachsen, Y.W., Rickard, L.V., and Offield, T.W., 1962, The geology of New York State: Albany, New York State Museum—Geological Survey, Map and Chart Series no. 5, 5 sheets, scale 1:250,000.

Cadwell, D.H., and Muller, E.H., 1986, Surficial geologic map of New York: Albany, New York State Museum—Geological Survey, Map and Chart Series no. 40, 5 sheets, scale 1:250,000, digital compilation by Beckie Ugolini, 1998, from New York State Geological Survey 90-meter Digital Elevation Model.

Cartwright, R.H., and J.A. Ziarno, 1980, Chemical quality of water from community systems in New York, November 1970 to May 1975: U.S. Geological Survey Water-Resources Investigations Report 80–77, 444 p.

Coates, D.R., 1966, Glaciated Appalachian Plateau—Till shadows on hills: Science, v. 152, p. 1617–1619.

Cosner, O.J., 1984, Atlas of four selected aquifers in New York: Washington, D.C., U.S. Environmental Protection Agency Report 68-01-6389, 102 p.

Crain, L.J., 1975, Chemical quality of groundwater in the western Oswego River Basin: New York State Department of Environmental Conservation, Basin Planning Report ORB-3, 69 p.

Eckhardt, D.A., Hetcher, K.K., Phillips, P.J., and Miller, T.S., 2001, Pesticides and their metabolites in community water-supply wells of central and central New York, August 1999: U.S. Geological Survey Water-Resources Investigations Report 00–4128, 12 p.

Eckhardt, D.A., Reddy, J.E., and Tamulonis, K.L., 2007, Groundwater quality in the Genesee River Basin, New York, 2005-06: U.S. Geological Survey Open-File Report 2007–1093, 26 p., available at *http://pubs.usgs.gov/of/2007/1093*.

Eckhardt, D.A., Reddy, J.E., and Tamulonis, K.L., 2008, Groundwater quality in western New York, 2007: U.S. Geological Survey Open-File Report 2008–1140, 36 p., available at *http://pubs.usgs.gov/of/2008/1140*.

Eckhardt, D.A. and Stackelberg, P.E., 1995, Relation of groundwater quality to land use of Long Island, New York: Groundwater, v. 33, no. 6, p. 1019-1033.

Fairchild, H.L., 1928, Geologic story of the Genesee Valley and drainage history of central New York: Rochester, Gas and Electric News, July 1926 to July 1928.

Furlong, E.T., Anderson, B.D., Werner, S.L., Soliven, P.P., Coffey, L.J., and Burkhardt, M.R., 2001, Methods of analysis by the U.S. Geological Survey National Water Quality Laboratory—Determination of pesticides in water by graphitized carbon-based solid-phase extraction and high-performance liquid chromatography/mass spectrometry: U.S. Geological Survey Water-Resources Investigations Report 01–4134, 73 p.

Hem, J.D., 1985, Study and interpretation of the chemical characteristics of natural water (3d ed.): U.S. Geological Survey Water-Supply Paper 2254, 264 p.

Hetcher-Aguila, K.K., 2004, Groundwater quality in the Chemung River Basin, New York, 2003: U.S. Geological Survey Open-File Report 2004–1329, 19 p., available at *http://ny.water.usgs.gov/pubs/of/of041329*.

Hetcher-Aguila, K.K. and Eckhardt, D.A., 2006, Groundwater quality in the upper Susquehanna River basin, New York, 2004-05: U.S. Geological Survey Open-File Report 2006–1161, 21 p., available at *http://pubs.usgs.gov/of/2006/1161*.

Isachsen, Y.W., Landing, Ed, Lauber, J.M., Rickard, L.V., and Rogers, W.B., 2000, Geology of New York: A simplified account (2d ed.): Albany, N.Y., New York State Museum/Geological Survey, 294 p.

Kantrowitz, I.H., 1970, Chemical quality of groundwater in the eastern Oswego River basin: New York State Department of Environmental Conservation, Basin Planning Report ORB-2, 129 p.

Kontis, A.L., Randall, A.D., and Mazzaferro, D.L., 2004, Regional hydrology and simulation of flow of stratified-drift aquifers in the glaciated northeastern United States: U.S. Geological Survey Professional Paper 1415-C, 156 p.

Lee, E.A., and Strahan, A.P., 2003, Determination of acetamide herbicides and their degradation products in water using online solid-phase extraction and liquid chromatography/mass spectrometry: U.S. Geological Survey Open-File Report 03–173, 17 p.

Meyer, M.T., Mills, M.S., and Thurman, E.M., 1993, Automated solid-phase extraction of herbicides from water for gas chromatographic-mass spectrometric analysis: Journal of Chromatography, v. 629, p. 55–59.

Miller, T.S., 1982, Geology and groundwater resources of Oswego County, New York: U.S. Geological Survey Water-Resources Investigations Report 81–60, 37 p.

Miller, T.S., 1988, Unconsolidated aquifers in upstate New York – Finger Lakes sheet: U.S. Geological Survey Water-Resources Investigations Report 87–4122, 1 sheet, scale 1:250,000.

Miller, T.S., 1990, Sand and gravel aquifers of Schuyler County, New York: U.S. Geological Survey Water-Resources Investigations Report 90–4073, 1 sheet, scale 1:48,000.

New York State Department of Health, 2007a, Public water systems – Codes, Rules, and Regulations: Troy, N.Y., Bureau of Public Water Supply Protection, accessed October 2007 at *http://www.health.state.ny.us/environmental/water/drinking/part5/subpart5.htm.*

New York State Department of Health, 2007b, Public water systems – Maximum Contaminant Levels: Troy, N.Y., Bureau of Public Water Supply Protection, accessed January 2009 at *http://www.health.state.ny.us/nysdoh/water/part5/tables.htm.*

Nystrom, E.A., 2006, Groundwater quality in the Lake Champlain basin, New York, 2004: U.S. Geological Survey Open-File Report 06–1088, 22 p., available at *http://pubs.usgs.gov/of/2006/1088.*

Nystrom, E.A., 2007a, Groundwater quality in the Delaware River basin, New York, 2001 & 2005-2006: U.S. Geological Survey Open-File Report 2007–1098, 37 p., available at *http://pubs.usgs.gov/of/2007/1098.*

Nystrom, E.A., 2007b, Groundwater quality in the St. Lawrence River basin, New York, 2005-2006: U.S. Geological Survey Open-File Report 2007-1066, 33 p., available at *http://pubs.usgs.gov/of/2007/1066.*

Nystrom, E.A., 2008, Groundwater quality in the Mohawk River basin, New York, 2006: U.S. Geological Survey Open-File Report 2008–1086, 33 p., available at *http://pubs.usgs.gov/of/2008/1086.*

Nystrom, E.A., 2009, Groundwater quality in the upper Hudson River basin, New York, 2007: U.S. Geological Survey Open-File Report 2009–1240, 37 p., available at *http://pubs.usgs.gov/of/2009/1240.*

Pagano, T.S., Terry, D.B., and Ingram, A.W., 1986, Geohydrology of the glacial outwash aquifer in the Baldwinsville area, Seneca River, Onondaga County, New York, 1998: U.S. Geological Survey Water-Resources Investigations Report 85–4094, 7 sheets, 1:24,000 scale.

Phillips, P.J., Eckhardt, D.A., Terracciano, S.A., and Rosenmann, L.R., 1999, Pesticides and their metabolites in wells of Suffolk County, New York, 1998: U.S. Geological Survey Water-Resources Investigations Report 99–4095, 12 p.

Randall, A.D., 2001, Hydrogeologic framework of stratified-drift aquifers in the glaciated Northeastern United States: U.S. Geological Survey Professional Paper 1415-B, 179 p.

Sandstrom, M.W., Stroppel, M.E., Foreman, W.T., and Schroeder, M.P., 2001, Methods of analysis by the U.S. Geological Survey National Water Quality Laboratory—Determination of moderate-use pesticides and selected degradates in water by C-18 solid-phase extraction and gas chromatography/mass spectrometry: U.S. Geological Survey Water-Resources Investigations Report 01–4098, 70 p.

Shelton, L.R., 1994, Field guide for collecting and processing stream-water samples for the National Water-Quality Assessment Program: U.S. Geological Survey Open-File Report 94–455, 42 p.

U.S. Department of Commerce, 2000, Redistricting Census 2000: Washington D.C., Bureau of the Census Geography Division, accessed January 2009 at *http://www.census.gov/geo/www/index.html*.

U.S. Environmental Protection Agency, 1997, Guidelines for preparation of the comprehensive state water quality assessments, 305(b) reports, and electronic updates: Washington, D.C., Office of Water, EPA 841-B-97-002A and EPA 841-B-97-002B, PL 95-217.

U.S. Environmental Protection Agency, 1998, National primary drinking water regulations–Disinfectants and disinfection byproducts: Washington, D.C., Federal Register, December 16, 1998, v. 63, no. 241, p. 69389-69476.

U.S. Environmental Protection Agency, 2002, Drinking-water advisory—Consumer acceptability advice and health effects analysis on sodium: Washington, D.C., Office of Water, EPA 822-R-02-032, 34 p.

U.S. Environmental Protection Agency, 2004, Proposed radon in drinking water rule: Washington, D.C., Office of Water, accessed January 2009 at *http://www.epa.gov/safewater/radon/proposal.html*.

U.S. Environmental Protection Agency, 2006, Drinking water standards and health advisories: Washington, D.C., Office of Water, EPA 822-R-06-013, 12 p.

U.S. Geological Survey, variously dated, National field manual for the collection of water-quality data: U.S. Geological Survey Techniques of Water-Resources Investigations, book 9, chap. A1-A9, available online at *http://pubs.water.usgs.gov/twri9A*.

U.S. Geological Survey, 2007, National Water Quality Laboratory, accessed January 2009 at *http://nwql.usgs.gov*.

Waller, R.M., and Finch, A.J., 1982, Atlas of eleven selected aquifers in New York: U.S. Geological Survey Open-File Report 82–553, 255 p.

Weist, W.G., and Geist, G.L., 1969, Water resources of the central New York region: New York State Conservation Department, Water Resources Commission Bulletin 64, 58 p.

Wilde, F.D., Radtke, D.B., Gibs, Jacob, and Iwatsubo, R.T., eds., 2004, Processing of water samples: U.S. Geological Survey Techniques of Water-Resources Investigations, book 9, chap. A5, variously paged.

Yager, R.M., Kappel, W.M., and Plummer, L.N., 2007, Halite brine in the Onondaga Trough near Syracuse, New York—Characterization and simulation of variable-density flow: U.S. Geological Survey Scientific Investigations Report 2007–5058, 40 p.

Zaugg, S.D., Sandstrom, M.W., Smith, S.G., and Fehlberg, K.M., 1995, Methods of analysis by the U.S. Geological Survey National Water Quality Laboratory—Determination of pesticides in water by C-18 solid-phase extraction and capillary-column gas chromatography with selective-ion monitoring: U.S. Geological Survey Open-File Report 95–181, 49 p.

Appendix

Table A1. Description of wells sampled in the central New York study area, 2007.

[Well locations are shown in figure 1. Well No.: Prefix denotes county: C, Cortland; CM, Chemung; CY, Cayuga; L, Lewis; M, Madison; MO, Monroe; OD, Onondaga; OE, Oneida; OT, Ontario, OW, Oswego; SE, Seneca; SY, Schuyler; TM, Tompkins; WN, Wayne; YT, Yates; number is local well-identification number assigned by U.S. Geological Survey. Basin: CLO, Central Lake Ontario; OSR, Oswego River; ONR, Oneida River; SR, Seneca River. Well type: P, Production well; R, Residential well. –, information not available]

Well No.	Date sampled	Basin	Well type	Well depth, in feet below land surface	Casing depth, in feet below land surface	Physiographic province
Sand and gravel wells						
C 1461	12/5/2007	SR	P	127	100	Appalachian Plateau
CY 10	12/4/2007	SR	P	31	22	Appalachian Plateau
CY 265	11/13/2007	CLO	P	50	50	Lake Ontario Lowland
CY 995	9/11/2007	SR	R	80	80	Appalachian Plateau
M 291	10/23/2007	ONR	R	45	45	Lake Ontario Lowland
MO 1560	8/29/2007	CLO	R	40	40	Lake Ontario Lowland
OE 1465	10/10/2007	ONR	R	40	40	Lake Ontario Lowland
OE 2848	10/10/2007	ONR	R	41	41	Lake Ontario Lowland
OT 1864	9/18/2007	SR	R	108	108	Appalachian Plateau
OW 454	9/5/2007	OSR	P	70	60	Lake Ontario Lowland
OW 503	12/19/2007	ONR	P	70	70	Lake Ontario Lowland
SE 828	11/28/2007	SR	R	40	40	Appalachian Plateau
SE 1017	8/23/2007	SR	R	45	45	Appalachian Plateau
SY 402	8/22/2007	SR	P	33	22	Appalachian Plateau
TM 2355	8/16/2007	SR	R	145	145	Appalachian Plateau
WN 593	10/31/2007	CLO	P	66	60	Lake Ontario Lowland
YT 585	9/26/2007	SR	R	39	25	Appalachian Plateau
Bedrock wells						
CM 949	9/19/2007	SR	R	99	73.5	Appalachian Plateau
CY 266	12/18/2007	SR	R	220	20	Appalachian Plateau
CY 380	9/11/2007	SR	R	33	20	Lake Ontario Lowland
L 304	10/2/2007	ONR	R	162	20	Tug Hill Upland
M 290	8/28/2007	ONR	R	300	50	Lake Ontario Lowland
OD 830	11/7/2007	ONR	R	102	29	Lake Ontario Lowland
OD 1366	10/3/2007	SR	R	82	20	Lake Ontario Lowland
OD 1870	11/12/2007	SR	R	247	60	Appalachian Plateau
OD 1900	8/28/2007	ONR	R	280	53	Appalachian Plateau
OT 1480	10/24/2007	SR	R	95	20	Appalachian Plateau
OW 798	11/7/2007	ONR	R	69	48	Lake Ontario Lowland
SE 794	10/3/2007	SR	R	40	26	Lake Ontario Lowland
SY 1064	8/23/2007	SR	R	112	16	Appalachian Plateau
TM 1018	8/16/2007	SR	R	200	50	Appalachian Plateau
TM 2448	12/17/2007	SR	R	140	–	Appalachian Plateau
WN 814	9/18/2007	CLO	R	124	56	Lake Ontario Lowland
WN 847	11/6/2007	SR	R	45	36.75	Lake Ontario Lowland
YT 515	10/30/2007	SR	R	203	19	Appalachian Plateau

Table A2. Compounds for which groundwater samples collected from wells in the central New York study area were analyzed but not detected, 2007.

[NWIS, USGS National Water Information System; µg/L, micrograms per liter]

NWIS parameter code	Constituent	Laboratory reporting level, micrograms per liter
	Trace elements in unfiltered water	
71900	Mercury	0.010
	Pesticides in filtered water	
04038	2-Chloro-6-ethylamino-4-amino-*s*-triazine (CEAT)	0.08
50470	2,4-D methyl ester	0.20
39732	2,4-D	0.02 - 0.04
38746	2,4-DB	0.02
82660	2,6-Diethylaniline	0.002
49308	3-Hydroxy carbofuran	0.020 - 0.040
49260	Acetochlor	0.006
61029	Acetochlor ethanesulfonic acid	0.02
61030	Acetochlor oxanilic acid	0.02
63782	Acetochlor second amide	0.02
62847	Acetochlor sulfynilacetic acid	0.02
49315	Acifluorfen	0.040 - 0.060
46342	Alachlor	0.005-0.006
61031	Alachlor oxanilic acid	0.02
63781	Alachlor second amide	0.02
62848	Alachlor sulfynilacetic acid	0.02
49313	Aldicarb sulfone	0.08
49314	Aldicarb sulfoxide	0.040 - 0.060
49312	Aldicarb	0.04 - 0.12
34253	*alpha*-HCH	0.002
82686	Azinphos-methyl	0.080 - 0.120
50299	Bendiocarb	0.04
82673	Benfluralin	0.004 - 0.006
50300	Benomyl	0.020 - 0.040
61693	Bensulfuron methyl	0.06
38711	Bentazon	0.02 - 0.04
04029	Bromacil	0.02 -0.04
49311	Bromoxynil	0.12
04028	Butylate	0.002 - 0.004
50305	Caffeine	0.04 - 0.06
82680	Carbaryl	0.060
82674	Carbofuran	0.020
61188	Chloramben methyl ester	0.10
50306	Chlorimuron	0.080
38933	Chlorpyrifos	0.005
82687	*cis*-Permethrin	0.010
49305	Clopyralid	0.06

Table A2. Compounds for which groundwater samples collected from wells in the central New York study area were analyzed but not detected, 2007.—Continued

[NWIS, USGS National Water Information System; µg/L, micrograms per liter]

NWIS parameter code	Constituent	Laboratory reporting level, micrograms per liter
	Pesticides in filtered water	
04041	Cyanazine	0.018 - 0.020
04031	Cycloate	0.02 - 0.06
49304	Dacthal monoacid	0.02
82682	DCPA	0.003
63778	Dechloroacetochlor	0.02
63777	Dechloroalachlor	0.02
63779	Dechlorodimethenamid	0.02
63780	Dechlorometolachlor	0.02
62170	Desulfinyl fipronil	0.012
39572	Diazinon	0.005
38442	Dicamba	0.04 - 0.08
49302	Dichlorprop	0.02 - 0.04
39381	Dieldrin	0.009 - 1.07
61951	Dimethenamid ethanesulfonic acid	0.02
62482	Dimethenamid oxanilic acid	0.02
61588	Dimethenamid	0.02
49301	Dinoseb	0.04
04033	Diphenamid	0.04
82677	Disulfoton	0.02 - 0.11
49300	Diuron	0.04
82668	EPTC	0.002
82663	Ethalfluralin	0.009
82672	Ethoprop	0.012
62169	Desulfinylfipronil amide	0.029
62167	Fipronil sulfide	0.013
62168	Fipronil sulfone	0.024
62166	Fipronil	0.016 - 0.020
61952	Flufenacet ethanesulfonic acid	0.02
62483	Flufenacet oxanilic acid	0.02
62481	Flufenacet	0.02
61694	Flumetsulam	0.06
38811	Fluometuron	0.04
04095	Fonofos	0.006 - 0.010
63784	Hydroxyacetochlor	0.02
63783	Hydroxyalachlor	0.02
63785	Hydroxymetolachlor	0.02
64045	Hydroxydimethenamid	0.02
50356	Imazaquin	0.04
61695	Imidacloprid	0.060
39341	Lindane	0.004 - 0.006

Table A2. Compounds for which groundwater samples collected from wells in the central New York study area were analyzed but not detected, 2007.—Continued

[NWIS, USGS National Water Information System; µg/L, micrograms per liter]

NWIS parameter code	Constituent	Laboratory reporting level, micrograms per liter
	Pesticides in filtered water	
82666	Linuron	0.060
39532	Malathion	0.016
38482	MCPA	0.06
38487	MCPB	0.06 - 0.20
50359	Metalaxyl	0.02 - 0.04
38501	Methiocarb	0.040
49296	Methomyl	0.060 - 0.120
82667	Methyl parathion	0.008
82630	Metribuzin	0.012
61697	Metsulfuron	0.07 - 0.14
82671	Molinate	0.002
61692	*N*-(4-Chlorophenyl)-*N'*-methylurea	0.14
82684	Napropamide	0.018
49294	Neburon	0.02
50364	Nicosulfuron	0.10
49292	Oryzalin	0.04
38866	Oxamyl	0.04 - 0.12
34653	*p,p'*-DDE	0.003
39542	Parathion	0.010
82669	Pebulate	0.004 - 0.008
82683	Pendimethalin	0.012 - 0.020
82664	Phorate	0.020 - 0.040
49291	Picloram	0.12
82676	Propyzamide	0.004
04024	Propachlor	0.006 - 0.010
62766	Propachlor ethanesulfonic acid	0.05
62767	Propachlor oxanilic acid	0.02
82679	Propanil	0.006 - 0.011
82685	Propargite	0.02 - 0.04
49236	Propham	0.040 - 0.060
50471	Propiconazole	0.04 - 0.06
38538	Propoxur	0.040
38548	Siduron	0.02 - 0.04
50337	Sulfometuron	0.060
82665	Terbacil	0.018 - 0.040
82675	Terbufos	0.01 - 0.02
82681	Thiobencarb	0.010
82678	Triallate	0.006
49235	Triclopyr	0.04 - 0.08
82661	Trifluralin	0.006

Table A2. Compounds for which groundwater samples collected from wells in the central New York study area were analyzed but not detected, 2007.—Continued

[NWIS, USGS National Water Information System; µg/L, micrograms per liter]

NWIS parameter code	Constituent	Laboratory reporting level, micrograms per liter
	Volatile organic and phenolic compounds, in unfiltered water	
77652	1,1,2-Trichloro-1,2,2-trifluoroethane (CFC-113)	0.1
34536	1,2-Dichlorobenzene	0.1
32103	1,2-Dichloroethane	0.2
34541	1,2-Dichloropropane	0.1
34566	1,3-Dichlorobenzene	0.1
34571	1,4-Dichlorobenzene	0.1
34301	Chlorobenzene	0.1
34668	Dichlorodifluoromethane	0.2
81576	Diethyl ether	0.2
81577	Diisopropyl ether	0.2
78032	Methyl *tert*-butyl ether	0.2
50005	Methyl *tert*-pentyl ether	0.2
77128	Styrene	0.1
50004	*tert*-Butyl ethyl ether	0.1
32102	Tetrachloromethane	0.2
34546	*trans*-1,2-Dichloroethene	0.1
34488	Trichlorofluoromethane	0.2
39175	Vinyl Choride	0.2
32730	Phenolic Compounds	4

Table A3. Physical properties of groundwater samples from the central New York study area, 2007.

[Well locations are shown in figure 1. Well No.: Prefix denotes county: C, Cortland; CM, Chemung; CY, Cayuga; L, Lewis; M, Madison; MO, Monroe; OD, Onondaga; OE, Oneida; OT, Ontario, OW, Oswego; SE, Seneca; SY, Schuyler; TM, Tompkins; WN, Wayne; YT, Yates; number is local well-identification number assigned by U.S. Geological Survey. mg/L, milligrams per liter; <, less than; µS/cm, microsiemens per centimeter at 25°Celsius; (00080), USGS National Water Information System (NWIS) parameter code; –, no data. **Bold** values exceed one or more drinking-water standards]

Well No.	Water color, filtered, platinum-cobalt units (00080)	Dissolved-oxygen concentration, field, mg/L (00300)	pH, field, standard units (00400)	Specific conductance, field, µS/cm (00095)	Water temperature, degrees Celsius (00010)	Hydrogen sulfide (71875)
Sand and gravel wells						
C 1461	5	9.1	7.3	483	8.3	Absent
CY 10	5	5.5	7.2	658	12.8	Absent
CY 265	8	7.6	7.7	315	10.0	Absent
CY 995	5	0.4	7.5	488	16.9	Absent
M 291	10	< 0.3	7.2	830	17.2	Absent
MO 1560	2	6.0	7.3	1,090	16.4	Absent
OE 1465	5	< 0.3	7.3	2,500	14.1	Present
OE 2848	5	< 0.3	7.3	534	17.7	Present
OT 1864	8	0.3	7.3	736	14.8	Absent
OW 454	5	0.3	7.5	1,060	13.4	Absent
OW 503	2	2.9	8.3	141	8.7	Absent
SE 828	5	4.5	7.2	602	14.6	Absent
SE 1017	5	0.4	7.1	1,300	18.7	Absent
SY 402	5	1.3	7.2	622	14.9	Present
TM 2355	5	6.4	7.6	339	19.4	Absent
WN 593	5	< 0.3	7.6	490	10.4	Present
YT 585	5	0.5	7.1	805	19.5	Absent
Bedrock wells						
CM 949	5	< 0.3	7.5	379	14.8	Present
CY 266	8	4.4	7.3	889	10.6	Absent
CY 380	2	3.5	7.1	654	18.7	Absent
L 304	2	1.9	7.3	309	14.8	Absent
M 290	2	5.0	7.3	1,060	23.2	Absent
OD 830	5	1.2	7.7	320	14.2	Absent
OD 1366	8	1.0	7.4	1,090	14.7	Absent
OD 1870	8	< 0.3	7.5	608	11.0	Present
OD 1900	5	< 0.3	7.7	500	16.5	Absent
OT 1480	10	< 0.3	6.8	401	13.7	Absent
OW 798	12	6.5	8.2	179	10.8	Absent
SE 794	5	1.8	7.0	1,540	19.6	Absent
SY 1064	5	0.5	7.5	444	19.5	Absent
TM 1018	5	< 0.3	7.8	950	21.5	Present
TM 2448	**25**	2.7	7.5	580	9.8	Absent
WN 814	5	0.4	7.5	301	18.4	Absent
WN 847	8	< 0.3	7.3	740	12.4	Present
YT 515	15	0.9	7.0	11,700	12.8	Absent

Table A4. Concentrations of inorganic constituents in groundwater samples from the central New York study area, 2007.

[Well locations are shown in figure 1. Well No.: Prefix denotes county: C, Cortland; CM, Chemung; CY, Cayuga; L, Lewis; M, Madison; MO, Monroe; OD, Onondaga; OE, Oneida; OT, Ontario, OW, Oswego; SE, Seneca; SY, Schuyler; TM, Tompkins; WN, Wayne; YT, Yates; number is local well-identification number assigned by U.S. Geological Survey. Acid-neutralizing capacity, unfiltered and alkalinity, filtered: Fixed-endpoint titration at pH 4.5. Bicarbonate, filtered: Calculated from alkalinity. mg/L, milligrams per liter; (00900), USGS National Water Information System (NWIS) parameter code; CaCO₃, calcium carbonate. **Bold** values exceed one or more drinking-water standards]

Well No.	Hardness, filtered, mg/L as CaCO₃ (00900)	Calcium, filtered, mg/L (00915)	Magnesium, filtered, mg/L (00925)	Potassium, filtered, mg/L (00935)	Sodium, filtered, mg/L (00930)	Acid-neutralizing capacity, unfiltered, mg/L as CaCO₃ (90410)	Alkalinity, filtered, mg/L as CaCO₃ (29801)
Sand and gravel wells							
C 1461	200	58.2	12.9	0.91	18.3	166	167
CY 10	320	91.1	22.2	1.74	14.2	273	273
CY 265	150	41.4	11.1	0.93	3.48	137	137
CY 995	210	45.4	22.3	1.62	21.8	240	241
M 291	320	78.0	30.7	0.80	47.6	310	309
MO 1560	280	74.0	23.0	1.51	**126**	283	283
OE 1465	430	93.8	47.8	5.62	**343**	264	263
OE 2848	260	51.4	31.9	4.68	13.7	290	290
OT 1864	400	94.2	39.8	1.08	6.79	298	299
OW 454	250	73.1	17.1	3.29	**111**	224	224
OW 503	68	18.2	5.46	0.41	1.20	64	64
SE 828	330	101	17.9	0.77	2.82	265	267
SE 1017	490	132	39.8	1.72	**87.9**	365	365
SY 402	200	62.3	11.8	2.37	42.9	163	162
TM 2355	150	42.7	10.7	0.83	13.3	161	163
WN 593	240	59.6	22.7	0.99	7.06	177	177
YT 585	420	105	38.1	1.31	8.82	313	314
Bedrock wells							
CM 949	140	39.7	10.0	0.88	28.9	177	178
CY 266	350	99.2	25.0	2.70	40.5	207	209
CY 380	340	88.1	28.8	4.62	3.10	291	292
L 304	150	35.5	14.9	1.21	5.81	151	152
M 290	540	162	33.7	1.25	14.6	239	240
OD 830	130	29.5	13.4	5.60	6.28	112	112
OD 1366	350	93.3	28.2	37.7	**95.1**	194	199
OD 1870	170	51.1	11.2	1.31	59.7	230	230
OD 1900	140	31.3	13.8	1.79	**65.1**	198	226
OT 1480	180	50.0	12.6	1.36	18.2	211	212
OW 798	84	15.0	11.3	0.65	2.14	83	83
SE 794	870	262	51.7	3.58	21.2	285	285
SY 1064	140	37.7	9.97	0.85	46.6	202	203
TM 1018	100	27.5	7.64	0.73	**159**	201	202
TM 2448	260	70.0	20.1	2.14	27.1	252	245
WN 814	140	37.9	11.0	3.46	6.35	135	136
WN 847	310	68.7	34.5	3.11	4.19	242	242
YT 515	1,700	489	115	7.47	**1,870**	608	608

Table A4. Concentrations of inorganic constituents in groundwater samples from the central New York study area, 2007.—Continued

[Well locations are shown in figure 1. Well No.: Prefix denotes county: C, Cortland; CM, Chemung; CY, Cayuga; L, Lewis; M, Madison; MO, Monroe; OD, Onondaga; OE, Oneida; OT, Ontario, OW, Oswego; SE, Seneca; SY, Schuyler; TM, Tompkins; WN, Wayne; YT, Yates; number is local well-identification number assigned by U.S. Geological Survey. Acid-neutralizing capacity, unfiltered and alkalinity, filtered: Fixed-endpoint titration at pH 4.5. Bicarbonate, filtered: Calculated from alkalinity. mg/L, milligrams per liter; (29805), USGS National Water Information System (NWIS) parameter code; CaCO$_3$, calcium carbonate. **Bold** values exceed one or more drinking-water standards]

Well No.	Bicarbonate, filtered, mg/L as CaCO$_3$ (29805)	Chloride, filtered, mg/L (00940)	Fluoride, filtered, mg/L (00950)	Silica, filtered, mg/L (00955)	Sulfate, filtered, mg/L (00945)	Residue on evaporation, at 180° Celsius, filtered, mg/L (70300)
Sand and gravel wells						
C 1461	203	33.0	E 0.07	7.33	14.0	267
CY 10	333	26.7	0.14	5.48	35.3	383
CY 265	167	5.23	< 0.12	9.33	12.8	165
CY 995	293	17.4	0.42	14.4	< .18	259
M 291	378	72.8	E 0.11	12.9	22.0	464
MO 1560	345	160	0.12	10.0	40.6	596
OE 1465	322	**663**	E .06	11.2	29.2	1,400
OE 2848	354	8.96	0.15	14.7	3.80	304
OT 1864	364	17.1	0.19	14.6	95.9	470
OW 454	273	190	0.11	11.6	16.5	557
OW 503	78	1.49	E 0.08	6.64	7.14	74
SE 828	323	6.98	E 0.10	7.60	26.1	348
SE 1017	445	135	0.10	12.0	139	822
SY 402	199	77.6	E 0.10	5.73	29.5	343
TM 2355	196	2.10	0.29	13.2	15.9	196
WN 593	216	16.4	0.27	9.29	55.2	296
YT 585	382	28.8	0.21	14.2	94.9	504
Bedrock wells						
CM 949	216	17.5	0.19	11.5	5.27	219
CY 266	253	48.2	0.19	7.15	160	541
CY 380	355	10.3	0.12	6.77	32.0	373
L 304	184	2.74	E 0.09	10.4	11.7	170
M 290	292	46.1	0.46	6.29	**269**	723
OD 830	137	14.0	E 0.11	7.67	26.6	181
OD 1366	237	159	0.92	7.77	217	789
OD 1870	281	38.7	E 0.11	8.30	27.2	321
OD 1900	242	6.11	0.45	9.33	40.8	294
OT 1480	257	1.50	0.19	13.9	9.04	234
OW 798	101	0.68	E 0.07	7.76	10.2	98
SE 794	348	38.2	0.20	5.88	**543**	1,180
SY 1064	246	13.5	0.31	9.58	18.5	269
TM 1018	245	179	0.43	6.95	0.44	510
TM 2448	307	15.6	0.20	14.6	47.9	334
WN 814	165	2.22	0.12	11.0	21.0	168
WN 847	295	54.8	0.25	13.9	76.6	478
YT 515	742	**3,380**	0.27	9.56	E 0.14	7,130

Table A5. Concentrations of nutrients and total organic carbon in groundwater samples from the central New York study area, 2007.

[Well locations are shown in figure 1. Well No.: Prefix denotes county: C, Cortland; CM, Chemung; CY, Cayuga; L, Lewis; M, Madison; MO, Monroe; OD, Onondaga; OE, Oneida; OT, Ontario, OW, Oswego; SE, Seneca; SY, Schuyler; TM, Tompkins; WN, Wayne; YT, Yates; number is local well-identification number assigned by U.S. Geological Survey. mg/L, milligrams per liter; N, nitrogen; P, phosphorus; <, less than; (00623), National Water Information System (NWIS) parameter code; E, estimated value—constituent was detected in the sample but with low or inconsistent recovery]

Well No.	Ammonia plus organic nitrogen, filtered, mg/L as N (00623)	Ammonia, filtered, mg/L as N (00608)	Nitrate plus nitrite, filtered, mg/L as N (00631)	Nitrite, filtered, mg/L as N (00613)	Orthophosphate, filtered, mg/L as P (00671)	Total organic carbon, unfiltered, mg/L (00680)
Sand and gravel wells						
C 1461	< 0.14	< 0.020	4.70	< 0.002	E 0.003	< 1.0
CY 10	< 0.14	< 0.020	2.79	< 0.002	E 0.004	< 1.0
CY 265	< 0.14	< 0.020	2.11	< 0.002	E 0.004	< 1.0
CY 995	0.28	0.282	< 0.06	E 0.002	0.024	1.2
M 291	< 0.14	E 0.017	< 0.04	< 0.002	E 0.004	2.4
MO 1560	< 0.10	< 0.020	0.58	< 0.002	E 0.005	1.8
OE 1465	0.22	0.141	< 0.04	E 0.002	E 0.005	1.2
OE 2848	0.37	0.335	< 0.04	< 0.002	0.011	1.2
OT 1864	E 0.05	0.043	< 0.06	< 0.002	0.007	1.1
OW 454	0.14	0.110	0.25	E 0.002	E 0.006	1.7
OW 503	< 0.14	< 0.020	0.25	< 0.002	E 0.003	< 1.0
SE 828	< 0.14	< 0.020	7.34	< 0.002	E 0.004	< 1.0
SE 1017	0.12	0.031	0.25	0.089	0.009	2.1
SY 402	E 0.06	E 0.020	0.51	0.003	0.007	1.5
TM 2355	0.16	0.151	< 0.06	< 0.002	0.031	< 1.0
WN 593	0.21	0.020	< 0.04	< 0.002	E 0.005	< 1.0
YT 585	E 0.09	E 0.020	< 0.06	< 0.002	0.008	< 1.0
Bedrock wells						
CM 949	0.18	0.176	< 0.06	< 0.002	0.047	< 1.0
CY 266	0.38	0.271	1.23	0.039	E 0.004	1.4
CY 380	E 0.09	< 0.020	5.35	E 0.001	E 0.005	1.7
L 304	< 0.14	< 0.020	0.65	< 0.002	E 0.004	< 1.0
M 290	< 0.10	< 0.020	1.30	< 0.002	E 0.004	1.1
OD 830	< 0.14	0.041	0.10	< 0.002	< 0.006	1.0
OD 1366	2.5	2.50	< 0.04	< 0.002	E 0.004	< 1.0
OD 1870	0.49	0.468	< 0.04	< 0.002	0.006	< 1.1
OD 1900	0.32	0.259	< 0.06	< 0.002	E 0.005	1.3
OT 1480	0.22	0.208	< 0.04	< 0.002	0.006	< 1.0
OW 798	< 0.14	< 0.020	0.08	< 0.002	E 0.003	< 1.0
SE 794	< 0.14	0.030	4.53	E 0.001	E 0.004	< 1.0
SY 1064	E 0.10	0.073	0.10	E 0.001	0.011	< 1.0
TM 1018	0.48	0.425	< 0.06	< 0.002	0.012	< 1.0
TM 2448	0.16	0.146	< 0.04	< 0.002	E 0.005	< 1.0
WN 814	E 0.05	0.047	0.07	< 0.002	0.006	< 1.0
WN 847	0.33	0.064	< 0.04	< 0.002	E 0.005	2.7
YT 515	4.5	4.33	< 0.04	E 0.001	0.034	1.7

Table A6. Concentrations of trace elements and radon-222 in groundwater samples from the central New York study area, 2007.

[Well locations are shown in figure 1. Well No.: Prefix denotes county: C, Cortland; CM, Chemung; CY, Cayuga; L, Lewis; M, Madison; MO, Monroe; OD, Onondaga; OE, Oneida; OT, Ontario, OW, Oswego; SE, Seneca; SY, Schuyler; TM, Tompkins; WN, Wayne; YT, Yates; number is local well-identification number assigned by U.S. Geological Survey. µg/L, micrograms per liter; (01105), USGS National Water Information System (NWIS) parameter code; <, less than; E, estimated value—constituent was detected in the sample but with low or inconsistent recovery. **Bold** values exceed one or more drinking-water standards]

Well number	Aluminum, unfiltered, µg/L (01105)	Antimony, unfiltered, µg/L (01097)	Arsenic, unfiltered, µg/L (01002)	Barium, unfiltered, µg/L (01007)	Beryllium, unfiltered, µg/L (01012)	Boron, filtered, µg/L (01020)	Cadmium, unfiltered, µg/L (01027)	Chromium, unfiltered, µg/L (01034)
Sand and gravel wells								
C 1461	< 4	< 0.1	< 0.60	30.8	< 0.04	12	< 0.01	E 0.26
CY 10	14	< 0.1	< 0.60	63.2	< 0.04	18	< 0.01	< 0.40
CY 265	< 4	< 0.1	< 0.60	164	< 0.04	11	< 0.01	E 0.32
CY 995	41	< 0.2	0.23	572	< 0.06	111	< 0.02	< 0.60
M 291	<4	< 0.1	< 0.60	365	< 0.04	24	< 0.01	< 0.40
MO 1560	<2	< 0.2	E 0.12	52.0	< 0.06	45	< 0.02	E 0.48
OE 1465	<8	< 0.3	< 1.2	462	< 0.08	60	0.06	< 0.80
OE 2848	E 3	< 0.1	< 0.60	215	< 0.04	85	< 0.01	< 0.40
OT 1864	<2	< 0.2	7.2	63.8	< 0.06	9.5	< 0.02	< 0.60
OW 454	E 2	< 0.2	E 0.19	630	< 0.06	20	E 0.01	< 0.60
OW 503	E 3	< 0.1	1.3	10.5	< 0.04	6.0	< 0.01	E 0.27
SE 828	24	0.2	< 0.60	55.6	< 0.04	21	< 0.01	< 0.40
SE 1017	< 2	< 0.2	0.71	66.7	< 0.06	31	< 0.02	< 0.60
SY 402	< 2	< 0.2	0.37	25.7	< 0.06	29	0.03	< 0.60
TM 2355	33	< 0.2	3.8	203	< 0.06	34	E0.01	< 0.60
WN 593	E 4	< 0.1	< 0.60	353	< 0.04	12	E 0.01	< 0.40
YT 585	4	< 0.2	2.3	39.7	< 0.06	14	0.02	< 0.60
Bedrock wells								
CM 949	15	< 0.2	E 0.13	911	< 0.06	62	< 0.02	< 0.60
CY 266	**4,830**	0.4	8.7	233	0.2	502	< 0.01	7.4
CY 380	E 2	< 0.2	E 0.17	94.0	< 0.06	24	< 0.02	< 0.60
L 304	**88**	E 0.1	E 0.49	148	< 0.04	30	E 0.01	E 0.32
M 290	9	E 0.2	0.25	81.6	< 0.06	46	< 0.02	< 0.60
OD 830	< 4	0.3	0.93	71.2	< 0.04	92	0.02	< 0.40
OD 1366	10	E 0.1	1.8	12.3	< 0.04	3,140	E 0.01	< 0.40
OD 1870	9	< 0.1	< 0.60	286	< 0.04	294	< 0.01	< 0.40
OD 1900	2	< 0.2	E 0.10	302	< 0.06	761	< 0.02	< 0.60
OT 1480	< 4	< 0.1	0.85	331	< 0.04	139	< 0.01	< 0.40
OW 798	5	< 0.1	1.1	21.9	< 0.04	5.0	< 0.01	0.43
SE 794	20	E 0.1	< 0.60	14.4	< 0.04	45	< 0.01	E 0.22
SY 1064	E 1	< 0.2	0.29	122	< 0.06	265	E 0.01	< 0.60
TM 1018	**256**	< 0.2	0.23	1,290	< 0.06	346	< 0.02	E 0.46
TM 2448	46	0.2	E 0.49	54.7	< 0.04	113	0.02	< 0.40
WN 814	E 2	< 0.2	3.1	60.8	< 0.06	38	< 0.02	< 0.60
WN 847	< 4	0.5	2.2	85.5	< 0.04	113	E 0.01	< 0.40
YT 515	E 15	< 0.7	< 3.0	**10,400**	< 0.20	872	< 0.07	44.4

Table A6. Concentrations of trace elements and radon-222 in groundwater samples from the central New York study area, 2007.—Continued

[Well locations are shown in figure 1. Well No.: Prefix denotes county: C, Cortland; CM, Chemung; CY, Cayuga; L, Lewis; M, Madison; MO, Monroe; OD, Onondaga; OE, Oneida; OT, Ontario; OW, Oswego; SE, Seneca; SY, Schuyler; TM, Tompkins; WN, Wayne; YT, Yates; number is local well-identification number assigned by U.S. Geological Survey. µg/L, micrograms per liter; (01037), USGS National Water Information System (NWIS) parameter code; <, less than; E, estimated value—constituent was detected in the sample but with low or inconsistent recovery; M, measured but not quantified. **Bold** values exceed one or more drinking-water standards]

Well number	Cobalt, unfiltered, µg/L (01037)	Copper, unfiltered, µg/L (01042)	Iron, filtered, µg/L (01046)	Iron, unfiltered, µg/L (01045)	Lead, unfiltered, µg/L (01051)	Lithium, unfiltered, µg/L (01132)	Manganese, filtered, µg/L (01056)	Manganese, unfiltered, µg/L (01055)	Molybdenum, unfiltered, µg/L (01062)
				Sand and gravel wells					
C 1461	< 0.04	< 1.2	< 8	< 6	2.00	5.0	< 0.4	<0.8	< 0.1
CY 10	E 0.02	2.7	< 8	< 6	0.23	2.7	< 0.4	< 0.8	0.6
CY 265	< 0.04	3.1	< 8	< 6	0.27	2.0	< 0.4	< 0.4	E 0.1
CY 995	0.06	3.4	**1,560**	**2,030**	2.11	42.7	16.4	19.4	0.5
M 291	< 0.04	< 1.2	**1,870**	**2,860**	0.32	5.1	**76.1**	**92.0**	0.3
MO 1560	< 0.04	1.7	30	199	0.60	3.8	8.7	15.4	M
OE 1465	< 0.08	14	< 24	158	E 0.08	26.6	**86.2**	**79.6**	0.5
OE 2848	< 0.04	< 1.2	**482**	**502**	0.25	22.3	42.8	44.0	0.3
OT 1864	0.12	< 1.2	**930**	**925**	0.06	6.1	29.1	32.9	0.8
OW 454	0.07	2.3	51	54	0.13	18.9	176	**178**	0.3
OW 503	< 0.04	< 1.2	< 8	9	0.43	1.3	< 0.4	< 0.4	< 0.1
SE 828	0.06	8.7	< 8	99	1.49	2.6	E .2	2.4	0.4
SE 1017	0.13	E .85	**1,930**	**1,790**	0.76	9.5	**85.0**	**94.1**	1.9
SY 402	E 0.02	10.6	11	25	0.16	5.1	20.8	21.4	0.5
TM 2355	E 0.02	< 1.2	250	**316**	1.14	7.9	**61.6**	**63.4**	3.5
WN 593	< 0.04	1.3	49	49	0.11	4.4	**58.9**	**66.2**	1.2
YT 585	0.17	E 0.72	**1,660**	**1,950**	0.08	17.2	33.2	37.3	2.5
				Bedrock wells					
CM 949	< 0.04	6.3	**414**	**438**	0.29	11.8	**56.2**	**60.4**	0.1
CY 266	4.70	4.5	< 8	**9,190**	4.00	44.7	3.1	**242**	2.0
CY 380	0.04	22.1	< 6	94	1.54	2.8	0.3	1.1	0.4
L 304	0.10	5.8	< 8	168	0.46	7.6	1.1	7.0	0.1
M 290	E 0.03	1.2	25	50	0.08	13.6	4.0	4.4	0.9
OD 830	< 0.04	1.9	47	< 6	0.08	24.3	3.6	3.5	1.0
OD 1366	0.14	E 0.61	96	130	0.31	383	18.9	21.2	1.4
OD 1870	< 0.04	4.4	34	98	0.30	123	**81.3**	**86.4**	0.2
OD 1900	E.02	E 0.90	8	26	E 0.04	113	4.0	3.6	0.2
OT 1480	0.08	<1.2	**452**	**532**	0.64	21.5	**300**	**330**	0.5
OW 798	< 0.04	E 1.2	15	**352**	1.01	2.7	4.4	5.6	0.2
SE 794	0.11	10.0	115	178	0.69	15.8	2.1	1.2	0.6
SY 1064	< 0.04	< 1.2	E 4	29	0.34	29.8	12.3	14.8	0.3
TM 1018	0.24	180	238	**1,660**	1.48	155	35.9	43.4	0.1
TM 2448	0.19	< 1.2	130	169	0.07	57.0	**119**	**110**	6.0
WN 814	E 0.03	1.2	12	226	0.59	6.5	20.9	21.6	0.5
WN 847	< 0.04	1.3	**666**	**669**	0.14	13.3	4.7	4.6	1.3
YT 515	0.62	E 3.6	**3,530**	**3,470**	< 0.30	1,900	**515**	**594**	1.0

Table A6. Concentrations of trace elements and radon-222 in groundwater samples from the central New York study area, 2007.—Continued

[Well locations are shown in figure 1. Well No.: Prefix denotes county: C, Cortland; CM, Chemung; CY, Cayuga; L, Lewis; M, Madison; MO, Monroe; OD, Onondaga; OE, Oneida; OT, Ontario, OW, Oswego; SE, Seneca; SY, Schuyler; TM, Tompkins; WN, Wayne; YT, Yates; number is local well-identification number assigned by U.S. Geological Survey. μg/L, micrograms per liter; (01067), USGS National Water Information System (NWIS) parameter code; <, less than; E, estimated value—constituent was detected in the sample but with low or inconsistent recovery; M, measured but not quantified. **Bold** values exceed one or more drinking-water standards]

Well number	Nickel, unfiltered, μg/L (01067)	Selenium, unfiltered, μg/L (01147)	Silver, unfiltered, μg/L (01077)	Strontium, unfiltered, μg/L (01082)	Thallium, unfiltered, μg/L (01059)	Radon-222, unfiltered, picocuries per liter (pCi/L) (82303)	Uranium, (natural), unfiltered, μg/L (28011)	Zinc, unfiltered, μg/L (01092)
Sand and gravel wells								
C 1461	0.18	E 0.04	< 0.02	97.2	< 0.08	550	0.137	< 2.0
CY 10	0.40	0.20	< 0.02	180	E 0.05	450	0.756	2.0
CY 265	0.16	E 0.05	< 0.02	116	< 0.08	450	0.117	5.1
CY 995	E 0.14	< 0.08	< 0.02	979	< 0.18	80	< 0.012	7.3
M 291	0.24	< 0.08	< 0.02	127	< 0.08	120	0.167	23.1
MO 1560	E 0.16	0.21	< 0.02	180	< 0.18	120	0.300	3.7
OE 1465	0.24	< 0.16	< 0.04	975	< 0.16	170	< 0.040	E 3.6
OE 2848	< 0.12	< 0.08	< 0.02	1,050	< 0.08	70	< 0.020	< 2.0
OT 1864	E0.13	< 0.08	< 0.02	360	< 0.18	350	0.595	2.8
OW 454	0.27	< 0.08	< 0.02	1,100	< 0.18	580	0.297	2.9
OW 503	0.23	< 0.08	< 0.02	32.9	< 0.08	260	0.047	2.2
SE 828	1.50	0.16	< 0.02	119	< 0.08	260	0.468	4.4
SE 1017	0.81	< 0.08	< 0.02	247	< 0.18	80	2.36	2.6
SY 402	E0.12	E 0.07	< 0.02	152	< 0.18	680	0.410	8.4
TM 2355	E 0.11	< 0.08	< 0.02	388	< 0.18	160	0.043	E 1.5
WN 593	0.12	< 0.08	< 0.02	178	< 0.08	80	0.331	E 1.8
YT 585	0.33	< 0.08	< 0.02	609	< 0.18	90	0.641	4.1
Bedrock wells								
CM 949	E 0.08	< 0.08	< 0.02	587	< 0.18	330	< .012	3.3
CY 266	10.6	E 0.05	< 0.02	657	< 0.08	70	0.257	19.4
CY 380	0.98	0.18	< 0.02	116	< 0.18	400	0.836	15.8
L 304	0.28	< 0.08	< 0.02	127	< 0.08	120	0.079	4.6
M 290	1.0	0.16	< 0.02	9,230	< 0.18	680	0.837	24.5
OD 830	0.40	E 0.05	< 0.02	2,000	< 0.08	1,000	0.791	6.8
OD 1366	0.29	< 0.08	< 0.02	4,020	< 0.08	220	0.069	74.9
OD 1870	0.19	< 0.08	< 0.02	2,420	< 0.08	80	0.150	4.0
OD 1900	0.31	0.73	< 0.02	2,230	< 0.18	80	0.032	9.8
OT 1480	0.20	< 0.08	< 0.02	414	< 0.08	350	0.041	3.1
OW 798	< 0.12	0.09	< 0.02	46.5	< 0.08	140	0.445	E 1.1
SE 794	1.30	0.24	< 0.02	1,660	< 0.08	200	0.515	4.7
SY 1064	< 0.16	< 0.08	< 0.02	406	< 0.18	220	0.236	33.5
TM 1018	0.48	< 0.08	< 0.02	1,430	< 0.18	280	0.018	4.6
TM 2448	1.50	5.9	< 0.02	4,450	< 0.08	90	28.3	< 2.0
WN 814	< 0.16	< 0.08	< 0.02	167	< 0.18	190	0.176	4.5
WN 847	0.16	< 0.08	0.06	53,800	< 0.08	740	0.266	39.2
YT 515	25.4	< 0.40	< 0.10	23,600	< 0.40	210	< .100	E 8.7

Table A7. Concentrations of pesticides detected in groundwater samples from the central New York study area, 2007.

[Well locations are shown in figure 1. Well No.: Prefix denotes county: C, Cortland; CM, Chemung; CY, Cayuga; L, Lewis; M, Madison; MO, Monroe; OD, Onondaga; OE, Oneida; OT, Ontario, OW, Oswego; SE, Seneca; SY, Schuyler; TM, Tompkins; WN, Wayne; YT, Yates; number is local well-identification number assigned by U.S. Geological Survey. μg/L, micrograms per liter; <, less than; (04040), USGS National Water Information System (NWIS) parameter code; CIAT, 2-Chloro-4-isopropylamino-6-amino-s-triazine; OIET, 2-Hydroxy-4-isopropylamino-6-ethylamino-s-triazine; ESA, ethanesulfanic acid; E, estimated value—constituent was detected in the sample but with low or inconsistent recovery; M, measured but not quantified; –, not analyzed]

Well No.	CIAT, filtered, μg/L (04040)	OIET filtered, μg/L (50355)	2-[(2-Ethyl-6-methylphenyl) amino]-2-oxo-ESA, filtered, μg/L (62850)	Alachlor ESA 2d amide filtered, μg/L (62849)	Alachlor ESA, filtered, μg/L (50009)	Imazethapyr filtered, μg/L (50407)	Atrazine, filtered, μg/L (39632)	Norflurazon filtered, μg/L (49293)
				Sand and gravel wells				
C 1461	E 0.003	< 0.040	< 0.02	< 0.02	0.02	< 0.04	< 0.007	< 0.02
CY 10	E 0.055	0.040	0.02	< 0.02	0.03	< 0.04	0.088	< 0.02
CY 265	E 0.024	< 0.040	< 0.02	0.02	0.76	< 0.04	0.018	< 0.02
CY 995	< 0.014	< 0.080	< 0.02	< 0.02	< 0.02	< 0.04	< 0.007	< 0.04
M 291	< 0.014	< 0.040	< 0.02	< 0.02	< 0.02	< 0.04	< 0.007	< 0.02
MO 1560	< 0.014	< 0.080	< 0.02	< 0.02	0.02	< 0.04	< 0.007	< 0.04
OE 1465	< 0.014	< 0.040	< 0.02	< 0.02	< 0.02	< 0.04	< 0.007	< 0.02
OE 2848	< 0.014	< 0.040	< 0.02	< 0.02	< 0.02	< 0.04	< 0.007	< 0.02
OT 1864	< 0.014	–	< 0.02	< 0.02	< 0.02	< 0.04	< 0.007	< 0.04
OW 454	E0 .009	< 0.080	< 0.02	< 0.02	< 0.02	< 0.04	0.023	< 0.04
OW 503	< 0.014	< 0.040	< 0.02	< 0.02	< 0.02	< 0.04	< 0.007	< 0.02
SE 828	E 0.023	< 0.040	< 0.02	< 0.02	< 0.02	< 0.04	< 0.007	< 0.02
SE 1017	< 0.014	< 0.080	< 0.02	< 0.02	< 0.02	< 0.04	< 0.007	< 0.04
SY 402	E 0.008	< 0.080	< 0.02	0.02	< 0.02	< 0.04	0.013	M
TM 2355	< 0.014	< 0.080	< 0.02	< 0.02	< 0.02	< 0.04	< 0.007	< 0.04
WN 593	E 0.001	< 0.040	< 0.02	< 0.02	0.15	< 0.04	< 0.007	< 0.02
YT 585	< 0.014	< 0.080	< 0.02	< 0.02	< 0.02	< 0.04	< 0.007	< 0.04
				Bedrock wells				
CM 949	< 0.014	–	< 0.02	< 0.02	< 0.02	< 0.04	< 0.007	< 0.04
CY 266	< 0.014	< 0.040	< 0.02	< 0.02	< 0.02	< 0.04	E 0.003	< 0.02
CY 380	E 0.075	< 0.080	< 0.02	< 0.02	< 0.02	< 0.04	0.011	< 0.04
L 304	< 0.014	< 0.040	< 0.02	< 0.02	< 0.02	< 0.04	< 0.007	< 0.02
M 290	< 0.014	< 0.080	< 0.02	< 0.02	< 0.02	< 0.04	< 0.007	< 0.04
OD 830	< 0.014	< 0.040	< 0.02	< 0.02	< 0.02	< 0.04	< 0.007	< 0.02
OD 1366	E 0.004	< 0.040	< 0.02	< 0.02	< 0.02	< 0.04	< 0.007	< 0.02
OD 1870	< 0.014	< 0.040	< 0.02	< 0.02	< 0.02	< 0.04	< 0.007	< 0.02
OD 1900	< 0.014	< 0.080	< 0.02	< 0.02	< 0.02	M	< 0.007	< 0.04
OT 1480	< 0.014	< 0.040	< 0.02	< 0.02	0.02	< 0.04	< 0.007	< 0.02
OW 798	< 0.014	< 0.040	< 0.02	< 0.02	< 0.02	< 0.04	< 0.007	< 0.02
SE 794	< 0.014	< 0.040	< 0.02	< 0.02	< 0.02	< 0.04	< 0.007	< 0.02
SY 1064	< 0.014	< 0.080	< 0.02	< 0.02	< 0.02	< 0.04	< 0.007	< 0.04
TM 1018	< 0.014	< 0.080	< 0.02	< 0.02	< 0.02	< 0.04	< 0.007	< 0.04
TM 2448	< 0.014	< 0.040	< 0.02	< 0.02	< 0.02	< 0.04	< 0.007	< 0.02
WN 814	< 0.014	–	< 0.02	< 0.02	< 0.02	< 0.04	< 0.007	< 0.04
WN 847	< 0.014	< 0.040	0.02	< 0.02	0.07	< 0.04	< 0.007	< 0.02
YT 515	–	< 0.040	< 0.02	< 0.02	< 0.02	< 0.04	–	< 0.02

Table A7. Concentrations of pesticides detected in groundwater samples from the central New York study area, 2007.—Continued

[Well locations are shown in figure 1. Well No.: Prefix denotes county: C, Cortland; CM, Chemung; CY, Cayuga; L, Lewis; M, Madison; MO, Monroe; OD, Onondaga; OE, Oneida; OT, Ontario, OW, Oswego; SE, Seneca; SY, Schuyler; TM, Tompkins; WN, Wayne; YT, Yates; number is local well-identification number assigned by U.S. Geological Survey. µg/L, micrograms per liter; <, less than; (49297), USGS National Water Information System (NWIS) parameter code; CIAT, 2-Chloro-4-isopropylamino-6-amino-s-triazine; OIET, 2-Hydroxy-4-isopropylamino-6-ethylamino-s-triazine; ESA, ethanesulfanic acid; E, estimated value—constituent was detected in the sample but with low or inconsistent recovery; M, measured but not quantified; –, not analyzed]

Well No.	Fenuron filtered, µg/L (49297)	Metola-chlor ESA, filtered, µg/L (61043)	Metola-chlor OA, filtered, µg/L (61044)	Metola-chlor, filtered, µg/L (39415)	Prometon filtered, µg/L (04037)	Simazine, filtered, µg/L (04035)	Tebuthiron filtered, µg/L (82670)
Sand and gravel wells							
C 1461	< 0.04	1.51	< 0.02	< 0.010	< 0.01	< 0.006	< 0.02
CY 10	< 0.04	0.68	0.22	E 0.006	0.03	0.006	< 0.02
CY 265	< 0.04	< 0.02	< 0.02	< 0.010	< 0.01	< 0.006	< 0.02
CY 995	0.05	< 0.02	< 0.02	< 0.010	< 0.01	< 0.006	< 0.02
M 291	< 0.04	< 0.02	< 0.02	< 0.010	< 0.01	< 0.006	< 0.05
MO 1560	< 0.04	< 0.02	< 0.02	< 0.010	< 0.01	< 0.006	< 0.02
OE 1465	< 0.04	< 0.02	< 0.02	< 0.010	< 0.01	< 0.006	< 0.02
OE 2848	< 0.04	< 0.02	< 0.02	< 0.010	< 0.01	< 0.006	< 0.02
OT 1864	< 0.04	< 0.02	< 0.02	< 0.010	< 0.01	< 0.006	< 0.02
OW 454	< 0.04	< 0.02	< 0.02	< 0.010	< 0.01	< 0.006	0.02
OW 503	< 0.04	< 0.02	< 0.02	< 0.010	< 0.01	< 0.006	< 0.02
SE 828	< 0.04	< 0.02	< 0.02	< 0.010	< 0.01	< 0.006	E 0.02
SE 1017	< 0.04	< 0.02	0.02	< 0.010	< 0.01	< 0.006	< 0.02
SY 402	< 0.04	< 0.02	< 0.02	< 0.010	< 0.01	0.011	< 0.02
TM 2355	< 0.04	< 0.02	< 0.02	< 0.010	< 0.01	< 0.006	< 0.02
WN 593	< 0.04	0.07	0.08	< 0.010	< 0.01	< 0.006	< 0.02
YT 585	< 0.04	< 0.02	< 0.02	< 0.010	< 0.01	< 0.006	< 0.02
Bedrock wells							
CM 949	< 0.04	< 0.02	< 0.02	< 0.010	< 0.01	< 0.006	< 0.02
CY 266	< 0.04	< 0.02	< 0.02	< 0.010	< 0.01	< 0.006	< 0.02
CY 380	< 0.04	< 0.02	< 0.02	< 0.010	< 0.01	< 0.006	< 0.02
L 304	< 0.04	< 0.02	< 0.02	< 0.010	< 0.01	< 0.006	< 0.02
M 290	< 0.04	< 0.02	< 0.02	< 0.010	< 0.01	< 0.006	< 0.02
OD 830	< 0.04	< 0.02	< 0.02	< 0.010	< 0.01	< 0.006	< 0.02
OD 1366	< 0.04	< 0.02	< 0.02	< 0.010	< 0.01	< 0.006	< 0.02
OD 1870	< 0.04	< 0.02	< 0.02	< 0.010	< 0.01	< 0.006	< 0.02
OD 1900	< 0.04	< 0.02	< 0.02	< 0.010	< 0.01	< 0.006	< 0.02
OT 1480	< 0.04	< 0.02	< 0.02	< 0.010	< 0.01	< 0.006	< 0.02
OW 798	< 0.04	< 0.02	< 0.02	< 0.010	< 0.01	< 0.006	< 0.02
SE 794	< 0.04	0.08	< 0.02	< 0.010	< 0.01	< 0.006	< 0.02
SY 1064	< 0.04	< 0.02	< 0.02	< 0.010	< 0.01	< 0.006	< 0.02
TM 1018	< 0.04	< 0.02	< 0.02	< 0.010	< 0.01	< 0.006	< 0.02
TM 2448	< 0.04	< 0.02	< 0.02	< 0.010	< 0.01	< 0.006	< 0.02
WN 814	< 0.04	< 0.02	< 0.02	< 0.010	< 0.01	< 0.006	< 0.02
WN 847	< 0.04	< 0.02	0.07	< 0.010	< 0.01	< 0.006	< 0.02
YT 515	< 0.04	< 0.02	< 0.02	< 0.010	< 0.01	–	–

Table A8. Concentrations of volatile organic compounds in groundwater samples from the central New York study area, 2007.

[Well locations are shown in figure 1. Well No.: Prefix denotes county: C, Cortland; CM, Chemung; CY, Cayuga; L, Lewis; M, Madison; MO, Monroe; OD, Onondaga; OE, Oneida; OT, Ontario; OW, Oswego; SE, Seneca; SY, Schuyler; TM, Tompkins; WN, Wayne; YT, Yates; number is local well-identification number assigned by U.S. Geological Survey. µg/L, micrograms per liter; <, less than; (34506), USGS National Water Information System parameter code; E, estimated value—constituent was detected in the sample but with low or inconsistent recovery. **Bold** values exceed one or more drinking-water standards]

Well No.	1,1,1-Trichloro-ethane, unfiltered, µg/L (34506)	1,1-Dichloro-ethane, unfiltered, µg/L (34496)	1,1-Dichloro-ethene, unfiltered, µg/L (34501)	Dichloro-methane, unfiltered, µg/L (34423)	Bromodichloro-methane, unfiltered, µg/L (32101)	Tribromo-methane, unfiltered, µg/L (32104)	Dibromo-chloro-methane, unfiltered, µg/L (32105)	Trichloro-methane, unfiltered, µg/L (32106)
Sand and gravel wells								
C 1461	< 0.1	<0.1	< 0.1	< 0.2	< 0.1	< 0.2	< 0.2	< 0.1
CY 10	< 0.1	< 0.1	< 0.1	< 0.2	0.3	< 0.2	0.2	0.4
CY 265	< 0.1	< 0.1	< 0.1	< 0.2	< 0.1	< 0.2	< 0.2	< 0.1
CY 995	< 0.1	< 0.1	< 0.1	< 0.2	< 0.1	< 0.2	< 0.2	< 0.1
M 291	< 0.1	< 0.1	< 0.1	< 0.2	< 0.1	< 0.2	< 0.2	0.5
MO 1560	< 0.1	< 0.1	< 0.1	< 0.2	< 0.1	< 0.2	< 0.2	<0.1
OE 1465	< 0.1	< 0.1	< 0.1	0.2	0.9	0.5	1.0	1.6
OE 2848	< 0.1	< 0.1	< 0.1	< 0.2	< 0.1	< 0.2	< 0.2	< 0.1
OT 1864	< 0.1	< 0.1	< 0.1	< 0.2	< 0.1	< 0.2	< 0.2	< 0.1
OW 454	2.0	0.3	0.4	< 0.2	< 0.1	< 0.2	< 0.2	< 0.1
OW 503	< 0.1	< 0.1	< 0.1	< 0.2	< 0.1	< 0.2	< 0.2	< 0.1
SE 828	< 0.1	< 0.1	< 0.1	< 0.2	< 0.1	< 0.2	< 0.2	< 0.1
SE 1017	< 0.1	< 0.1	< 0.1	< 0.2	< 0.1	< 0.2	< 0.2	< 0.1
SY 402	< 0.1	< 0.1	< 0.1	< 0.2	< 0.1	< 0.2	< 0.2	< 0.1
TM 2355	< 0.1	< 0.1	< 0.1	< 0.2	< 0.1	< 0.2	< 0.2	< 0.1
WN 593	< 0.1	< 0.1	< 0.1	< 0.2	< 0.1	< 0.2	< 0.2	< 0.1
YT 585	< 0.1	< 0.1	< 0.1	< 0.2	< 0.1	< 0.2	< 0.2	< 0.1
Bedrock wells								
CM 949	< 0.1	< 0.1	< 0.1	< 0.2	< 0.1	< 0.2	< 0.2	< 0.1
CY 266	< 0.1	< 0.1	< 0.1	< 0.2	0.4	< 0.2	E 0.1	3.7
CY 380	< 0.1	< 0.1	< 0.1	< 0.2	< 0.1	< 0.2	< 0.2	< 0.1
L 304	< 0.1	< 0.1	< 0.1	< 0.2	< 0.1	< 0.2	< 0.2	< 0.1
M 290	< 0.1	< 0.1	< 0.1	< 0.2	< 0.1	< 0.2	< 0.2	< 0.1
OD 830	< 0.1	< 0.1	< 0.1	< 0.2	< 0.1	< 0.2	< 0.2	< 0.1
OD 1366	< 0.1	< 0.1	< 0.1	< 0.2	< 0.1	< 0.2	< 0.2	< 0.1
OD 1870	< 0.1	< 0.1	< 0.1	< 0.2	< 0.1	< 0.2	< 0.2	< 0.1
OD 1900	< 0.1	< 0.1	< 0.1	< 0.2	< 0.1	< 0.2	< 0.2	0.7
OT 1480	< 0.1	< 0.1	< 0.1	< 0.2	< 0.1	< 0.2	< 0.2	< 0.1
OW 798	< 0.1	< 0.1	< 0.1	< 0.2	< 0.1	< 0.2	< 0.2	< 0.1
SE 794	< 0.1	< 0.1	< 0.1	< 0.2	< 0.1	< 0.2	< 0.2	< 0.1
SY 1064	< 0.1	< 0.1	< 0.1	< 0.2	< 0.1	< 0.2	< 0.2	< 0.1
TM 1018	< 0.1	< 0.1	< 0.1	< 0.2	< 0.1	< 0.2	< 0.2	< 0.1
TM 2448	< 0.1	< 0.1	< 0.1	< 0.2	< 0.1	< 0.2	< 0.2	< 0.1
WN 814	< 0.1	< 0.1	< 0.1	< 0.2	< 0.1	< 0.2	< 0.2	< 0.1
WN 847	< 0.1	< 0.1	< 0.1	< 0.2	< 0.1	< 0.2	< 0.2	< 0.1
YT 515	< 0.1	< 0.1	< 0.1	< 0.2	< 0.1	< 0.2	< 0.2	< 0.1

Table A8. Concentrations of volatile organic compounds in groundwater samples from the central New York study area, 2007.—Continued

[Well locations are shown in figure 1. Well No.: Prefix denotes county: C, Cortland; CM, Chemung; CY, Cayuga; L, Lewis; M, Madison; MO, Monroe; OD, Onondaga; OE, Oneida; OT, Ontario, OW, Oswego; SE, Seneca; SY, Schuyler; TM, Tompkins; WN, Wayne; YT, Yates; number is local well-identification number assigned by U.S. Geological Survey. µg/L, micrograms per liter; <, less than; (34371), USGS National Water Information System parameter code; E, estimated value—constituent was detected in the sample but with low or inconsistent recovery. **Bold** values exceed one or more drinking-water standards]

Well No.	Ethyl-benzene, unfiltered, µg/L (34371)	Benzene unfiltered, µg/L (34030)	Toluene, unfiltered, µg/L (34010)	m- + p-Xylene, unfiltered, µg/L (85795)	o-Xylene, unfiltered, µg/L (77135)	cis-1,2 Dichloro-ethene, unfiltered, µg/L (77093)	Trichloro-ethene, unfiltered, µg/L (39180)	Tetrachloro-ethene, unfiltered, µg/L (34475)
				Sand and gravel wells				
C 1461	< 0.1	< 0.1	< 0.1	< 0.2	< 0.1	< 0.1	< 0.1	< 0.1
CY 10	< 0.1	< 0.1	< 0.1	< 0.2	< 0.1	< 0.1	< 0.1	< 0.1
CY 265	< 0.1	< 0.1	< 0.1	< 0.2	< 0.1	< 0.1	< 0.1	< 0.1
CY 995	< 0.1	< 0.1	0.8	< 0.2	< 0.1	< 0.1	< 0.1	< 0.1
M 291	< 0.1	< 0.1	0.2	< 0.2	< 0.1	< 0.1	< 0.1	< 0.1
MO 1560	< 0.1	< 0.1	< 0.1	< 0.2	< 0.1	< 0.1	< 0.1	< 0.1
OE 1465	< 0.1	< 0.1	< 0.1	< 0.2	< 0.1	< 0.1	< 0.1	< 0.1
OE 2848	< 0.1	< 0.1	0.1	< 0.2	< 0.1	< 0.1	< 0.1	< 0.1
OT 1864	< 0.1	< 0.1	< 0.1	< 0.2	< 0.1	< 0.1	< 0.1	< 0.1
OW 454	< 0.1	< 0.1	< 0.1	< 0.2	< 0.1	< 0.1	< 0.1	1.5
OW 503	< 0.1	< 0.1	< 0.1	< 0.2	< 0.1	< 0.1	< 0.1	< 0.1
SE 828	< 0.1	< 0.1	< 0.1	< 0.2	< 0.1	< 0.1	< 0.1	< 0.1
SE 1017	< 0.1	< 0.1	0.3	< 0.2	< 0.1	< 0.1	< 0.1	< 0.1
SY 402	< 0.1	< 0.1	< 0.1	< 0.2	< 0.1	< 0.1	< 0.1	< 0.1
TM 2355	< 0.1	< 0.1	< 0.1	< 0.2	< 0.1	< 0.1	< 0.1	< 0.1
WN 593	< 0.1	< 0.1	< 0.1	< 0.2	< 0.1	< 0.1	< 0.1	< 0.1
YT 585	< 0.1	< 0.1	< 0.1	< 0.2	< 0.1	< 0.1	< 0.1	< 0.1
				Bedrock wells				
CM 949	< 0.1	< 0.1	< 0.1	< 0.2	< 0.1	< 0.1	< 0.1	< 0.1
CY 266	< 0.1	< 0.1	< 0.1	< 0.2	< 0.1	< 0.1	< 0.1	< 0.1
CY 380	< 0.1	< 0.1	< 0.1	< 0.2	< 0.1	< 0.1	< 0.1	< 0.1
L 304	< 0.1	< 0.1	< 0.1	< 0.2	< 0.1	< 0.1	< 0.1	< 0.1
M 290	< 0.1	< 0.1	0.4	< 0.2	< 0.1	< 0.1	< 0.1	< 0.1
OD 830	< 0.1	< 0.1	< 0.1	< 0.2	< 0.1	< 0.1	< 0.1	< 0.1
OD 1366	< 0.1	< 0.1	0.1	< 0.2	< 0.1	< 0.1	< 0.1	< 0.1
OD 1870	< 0.1	< 0.1	< 0.1	< 0.2	< 0.1	< 0.1	< 0.1	< 0.1
OD 1900	< 0.1	< 0.1	< 0.1	< 0.2	< 0.1	< 0.1	< 0.1	< 0.1
OT 1480	< 0.1	< 0.1	< 0.1	< 0.2	< 0.1	< 0.1	< 0.1	< 0.1
OW 798	< 0.1	< 0.1	< 0.1	< 0.2	< 0.1	< 0.1	< 0.1	< 0.1
SE 794	< 0.1	< 0.1	< 0.1	< 0.2	< 0.1	0.4	**50.8**	< 0.1
SY 1064	< 0.1	< 0.1	0.2	< 0.2	< 0.1	< 0.1	< 0.1	< 0.1
TM 1018	< 0.1	< 0.1	< 0.1	< 0.2	< 0.1	< 0.1	< 0.1	< 0.1
TM 2448	< 0.1	< 0.1	1.0	< 0.2	< 0.1	< 0.1	< 0.1	< 0.1
WN 814	< 0.1	< 0.1	< 0.1	< 0.2	< 0.1	< 0.1	< 0.1	< 0.1
WN 847	< 0.1	< 0.1	< 0.1	< 0.2	< 0.1	< 0.1	< 0.1	< 0.1
YT 515	0.1	0.3	0.7	1.4	0.4	< 0.1	< 0.1	< 0.1

Table A9. Concentrations of bacteria in unfiltered groundwater samples from the central New York study area, 2007.

[Well locations are shown in figure 1. Well No.: Prefix denotes county: C, Cortland; CM, Chemung; CY, Cayuga; L, Lewis; M, Madison; MO, Monroe; OD, Onondaga; OE, Oneida; OT, Ontario, OW, Oswego; SE, Seneca; SY, Schuyler; TM, Tompkins; WN, Wayne; YT, Yates; number is local well-identification number assigned by U.S. Geological Survey. mL, milliliter; <, less than; > greater than; CFU, colony-forming unit; (61213), National Water Information System (NWIS) parameter code. **Bold** values exceed one or more drinking-water standards]

Well No.	Total coliform colonies per 100 mL (61213)	Fecal coliform colonies per 100 mL (61215)	*Escherichia coli,* colonies per 100 mL (31691)	Heterotrophic plate count, CFUs per mL (31692)
Sand and gravel wells				
C 1461	< 1	< 1	< 1	10
CY 10	< 1	< 1	< 1	4
CY 265	< 1	< 1	< 1	1
CY 995	**> 200**	< 1	< 1	269
M 291	**8**	< 1	< 1	9
MO 1560	**11**	< 1	< 1	41
OE 1465	< 1	< 1	< 1	< 1
OE 2848	< 1	< 1	< 1	4
OT 1864	< 1	< 1	< 1	10
OW 454	< 1	< 1	< 1	2
OW 503	< 1	< 1	< 1	6
SE 828	**> 200**	< 1	< 1	92
SE 1017	< 1	< 1	< 1	100
SY 402	< 1	< 1	< 1	1
TM 2355	< 1	< 1	< 1	4
WN 593	**26**	< 1	< 1	6
YT 585	**1**	< 1	< 1	4
Bedrock wells				
CM 949	< 1	< 1	< 1	19
CY 266	**88**	< 1	< 1	**926**
CY 380	**21**	< 1	< 1	27
L 304	**2**	< 1	< 1	8
M 290	**> 200**	< 1	< 1	**1,780**
OD 830	**2**	< 1	< 1	3
OD 1366	**> 200**	**2**	< 1	120
OD 1870	**50**	< 1	< 1	313
OD 1900	< 1	< 1	< 1	6
OT 1480	**25**	< 1	< 1	7
OW 798	**2**	< 1	< 1	22
SE 794	**> 200**	< 1	< 1	13
SY 1064	**10**	< 1	< 1	26
TM 1018	< 1	< 1	< 1	5
TM 2448	**31**	< 1	< 1	**6,880**
WN 814	**98**	< 1	< 1	26
WN 847	< 1	< 1	< 1	23
YT 515	< 1	< 1	< 1	4